History in Focus

GCSE

MODERN WORLD

History

TEACHER'S RESOURCE BOOK

BEN WALSH

JOHN MURRAY

Other titles in the series

GCSE British Social and Economic History
Pupil's Book 0 7195 7271 1
Teacher's Resource Book 0 7195 7272 X

By the same author

History Revision: GCSE Modern World History by Ben Walsh and Wayne Birks   0 7195 7055 7
Revision for History: GCSE Modern World History by Ben Walsh and Wayne Birks   0 7195 7229 0

First published in 1996
by John Murray (Publishers) Ltd
50 Albemarle Street
London W1X 4BD

Reprinted 1997 (with revisions) (twice), 1998 (twice), 1999 (twice), 2000

Layouts by Rachel Griffin
Illustrations by Tom Cross, Karen Donnelly and Mike Humphries
Cover photograph reproduced by courtesy of Popperfoto
Cover design by John Townson/Creation
Printed and bound in Great Britain by Rowland Digital, Bury St Edmunds, Suffolk

A CIP catalogue record for this book is available from the British Library.

Pupil's Book 0 7195 7231 2
Teacher's Resource Book 0 7195 7232 0

Contents

Introduction

The aims of the Teacher's Resource Book

This Teacher's Resource Book is intended to help teachers to get the most from their pupils as they use *GCSE Modern World History*. It provides a range of additional support materials which can be used alongside the Pupil's Book together with advice on planning pupils' routes through topics, and teaching a Modern World History course.

The new GCSE syllabuses

The revisions which have been made to GCSE syllabuses for the 1998 examinations have, predictably, brought new opportunities, but also new challenges. It is also fair to say that many old challenges, such as effective differentiation, still remain. The pupil's books in the *History in Focus* series aim to give pupils and teachers both an inspiring resource and a stimulating route through some of the most interesting stories and issues which History has to offer. Later sections of this introduction describe the key features of the Pupil's Book and how it interacts with the Teacher's Resource Book. This opening section deals with some broader issues surrounding GCSE Modern World History, and sets out the policies we have adopted to help teachers meet the challenges and address the issues.

Prescribed content

The new syllabuses differ to a limited extent from earlier syllabuses. They continue to identify clearly the key issues which underpin pupils' understanding of the momentous events under study. However, they prescribe more narrowly the content to be studied. Clearly this removes from the teacher the need to decide which content areas are to be covered. For some teachers, it will mean an increased amount of material to cover and for others it may mean less. The clear policy in the Pupil's Book has been to provide coverage of all the core areas of study in the major syllabuses. In addition, this coverage, wherever possible, tries to strike a realistic balance between the needs of pupils for depth of information, and the needs of teachers who are hard pressed to cover a course in five terms.

Assessment objectives

The assessment objectives across the new syllabuses are virtually identical.
The MEG Modern World History objectives read as follows:

Objective 1
Recall, select, organise and deploy knowledge of the syllabus content.

Objective 2
Describe, analyse and explain
• the events, changes and issues studied
• the key features of the periods, people, societies or situations studied.

Objective 3
In relation to the historical context:
• Comprehend, analyse and evaluate representations and interpretations of the events, people and issues studied.
• Comprehend, interpret, evaluate and use a range of sources of information of different types.

Pupils could do worse than spend their first GCSE History lesson looking at syllabus objectives and re-writing them in their own words. By doing so, they take hold of the terms and concepts. In their own minds pupils can turn these from words into actions.

The key to examination success, but also to a good understanding of history, is for teaching to be focused on pupils' progression in these assessment objectives. Above all, pupils must be able to do two things:

1 They must be able to **write at length**, and their writing must be informed and substantiated and must also meet the requirements of the task to which it is being addressed.
2 Pupils must **make reasoned judgements** about the use and value of source material, primary and secondary, by using the content and the context of that material.

These are formidable skills and few pupils will emerge from Key Stage 3 fully equipped in these areas. With this in mind, the majority of the Focus Tasks in the book broadly target one of these two abilities. In particular the worksheets which accompany the Focus Tasks are designed to act as a 'scaffolding' for all pupils' extended writing. As they grow in capability and confidence, more pupils will be able to work without the scaffolding.

How this course supports differentiated teaching and learning

Recent research from the USA into how the brain works and how learners learn has confirmed what most teachers know from experience:

- Different pupils learn in different ways and need to be catered for accordingly.
- Learning is more effective when it is active, and pupils are asked to do things with the information they find or are given.

The Pupil's Book and Teacher's Resource Book address this issue in a number of ways:

1 Through a variety of approaches to presenting information.
2 Through questions and activities which allow a flexibility of response, oral or written.
3 With tasks which demand that pupils process information rather than simply transfer it from one place to another (e.g. textbook to exercise book).
4 Perhaps most importantly, through stepped questions and activities which equip pupils to deal with the Focus Tasks which 'pull together' the key concepts and information in a particular section.

Example 1 Pages 299–305 of Chapter 12 deal with the Vietnam War in the context of the USA's policy of containment.

The aim of the Focus Task on page 305 is to investigate why the USA lost the Vietnam War. How might you use this material to prepare pupils for this challenge?

---

1 Teacher directs pupils to Focus Task – 'advance reminder'

↓

2 Reading through background on pages 299-300 as whole class(?)

↓

3 Class discussion of question 2, page 301, on source showing Viet Cong tactics

↓

4 After more class reading of page 301, small-group discussion and feedback on lists of problems faced by US troops – notes kept in rough

↓

5 Further reading together of 'the story' (pages 302–304) – class discussion of questions 1–3 (page 304) on My Lai Massacre

↓

6 Poster activity (page 304) which requires pupils to think through internal US opposition to war. They use Worksheet 12.6.

7 Focus Task. Worksheets 12.7a and b support this.

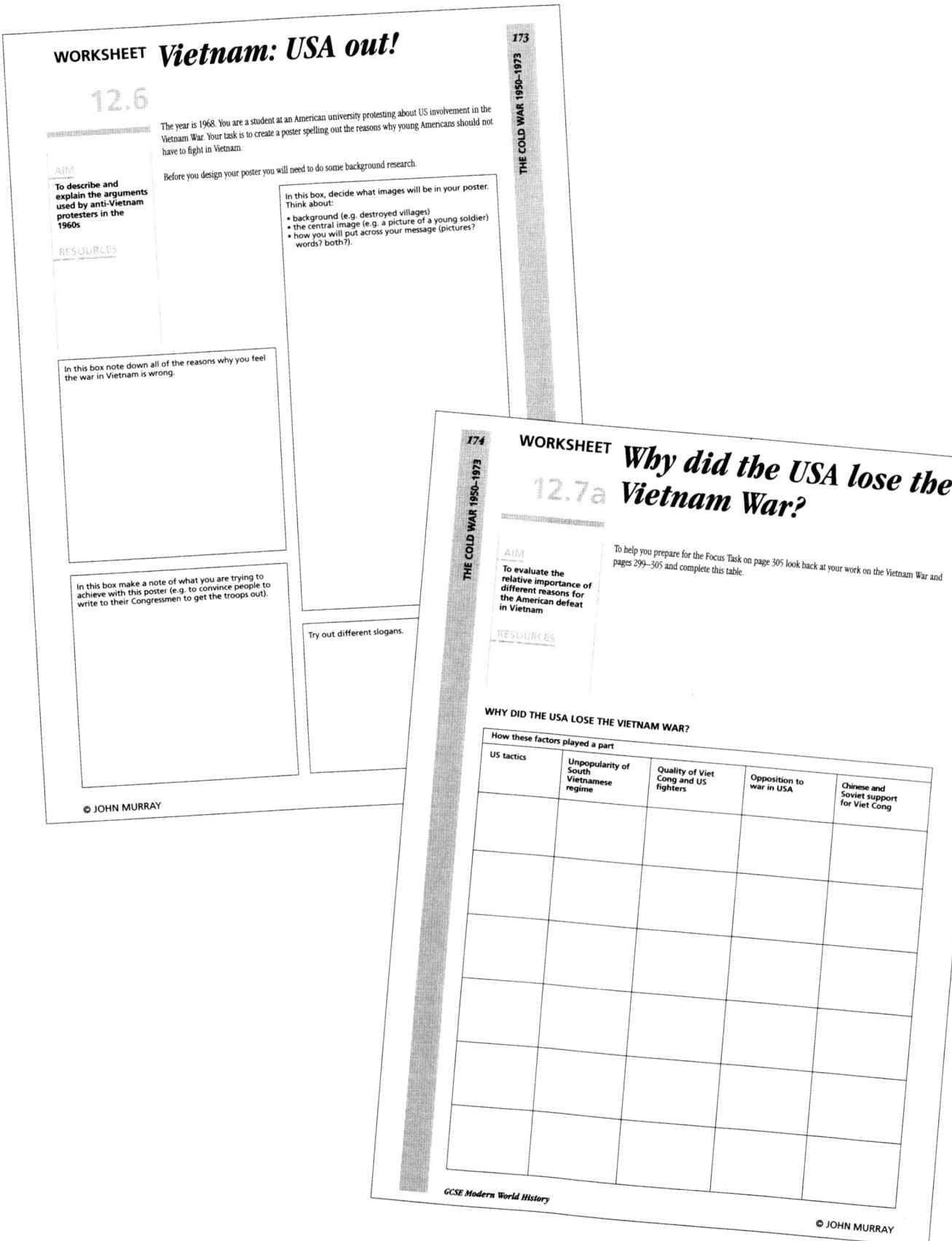

WORKSHEET *Vietnam: USA out!*

173

THE COLD WAR 1950–1973

12.6

AIM

To describe and explain the arguments used by anti-Vietnam protesters in the 1960s

RESOURCES

The year is 1968. You are a student at an American university protesting about US involvement in the Vietnam War. Your task is to create a poster spelling out the reasons why young Americans should not have to fight in Vietnam.

Before you design your poster you will need to do some background research.

In this box, decide what images will be in your poster. Think about:
• background (e.g. destroyed villages)
• the central image (e.g. a picture of a young soldier)
• how you will put across your message (pictures? words? both?).

In this box note down all of the reasons why you feel the war in Vietnam is wrong.

In this box make a note of what you are trying to achieve with this poster (e.g. to convince people to write to their Congressmen to get the troops out).

Try out different slogans.

© JOHN MURRAY

174

THE COLD WAR 1950–1973

WORKSHEET *Why did the USA lose the Vietnam War?*

12.7a

AIM

To evaluate the relative importance of different reasons for the American defeat in Vietnam

RESOURCES

To help you prepare for the Focus Task on page 305 look back at your work on the Vietnam War and pages 299–305 and complete this table.

WHY DID THE USA LOSE THE VIETNAM WAR?

| US tactics | Unpopularity of South Vietnamese regime | Quality of Viet Cong and US fighters | Opposition to war in USA | Chinese and Soviet support for Viet Cong |
How these factors played a part				

GCSE Modern World History

© JOHN MURRAY

(i) Pupils use Worksheets 12.7a and b to organise their ideas into a structure – translating a difficult idea and lots of content into a visual image.

(ii) Pupils then process this information into another diagram. Visual base helps them to link and categorise causes, physically making them larger or smaller and/or pointing out links with lines.

In this instance all pupils can achieve something through the comparatively non-threatening visual medium. However, more able pupils could easily be stretched by being given some extended written work. The boxes form handy paragraph headings and a final paragraph could be devoted to explaining causal links or 'families' of causes. Pupils needing extra support could be given a 'frame' for their writing, such as the one below. The use of such devices in tackling Focus Tasks is suggested throughout this Teacher's Resource Book.

Why did the USA lose the Vietnam War?

The issue we are discussing is whether one or more of these causes was the reason why the USA lost the war:

1 The USA's military tactics were not totally effective. For example …

2 The South Vietnamese regime was not popular because … This helped the Viet Cong …

3

4

5 Also, many of these factors worked together. For example …

Therefore, my conclusion is that many factors came together …
However, I feel that … were the most important because …

The essence of writing frames is that they build confidence. Teachers can add more or less in the way of clues and prompts, depending on the abilities of pupils. They do discourage copying and they force students to think in terms of headings, categories and paragraphs. However, it must be stressed that piece by piece this support needs to be removed. By the end of the GCSE course, the aim should be for pupils to devise their own structure.

Example 2

This task, on page 13 of Chapter 1, uses similar strategies but focuses more specifically on pupils using sources. In this instance, the topic is the origins of the Great War.

The issue in question is whether Germany started the war and should be held responsible for it. The knowledge and understanding base is gained from the preceding Focus Tasks in the chapter but this particular task is based on extracts from primary and secondary sources.

In many source-based tasks, pupils are given sources, asked to formulate a judgement on an issue and instructed to use the sources to support that judgement. This raises some problems:

1 Frequently, the information overload is more than their short-term memory can absorb.
2 Pupils find the generating of opinions extremely difficult.
3 Pupils find working with sources in an abstract task very difficult.

This Focus Task exemplifies the policies used throughout the book to overcome these problems:

1 Frameworks for recording interim ideas are provided to translate complex ideas into a more accessible format.
2 Opinions are provided, either to support, challenge or choose between. Weaker pupils therefore have something to work from. Able pupils can generate their own opinions or synthesise those provided.
3 Wherever possible, a context (e.g. the court case) is provided, so that pupils can anchor conceptual work in a real-world situation.

Like the 'non-source'-based exercises, these tasks require balanced and substantiated writing and a writing frame is again provided for pupils needing that support.

WORKSHEET *Was Germany to blame*
1.7 *for the war?*

AIM

To use a range of sources to compare different interpretations of the outbreak of war

RESOURCES

Your task is to look over the evidence and hold a re-trial, looking back from today. You will study evidence and hear from witnesses. You must then reach one of these four verdicts:

Verdict 1 Germany was rightly blamed for starting the war.
Verdict 2 Germany was mainly responsible for starting the war but the other powers should accept some of the blame.
Verdict 3 All of the major powers helped start the war. They should share the blame.
Verdict 4 No-one was to blame. The powers were swept along towards an inevitable war. It could not be stopped.

The table will help you as you examine the evidence presented by the witnesses.

Witness	1	2	3	4	5	6	7	8
Witness (Who?)								
Which verdict?								
What evidence?								
Can I trust the witness? Date and origin? Involved? Valuable? Reliable?								
Corroborated (backed up) by other sources?								
Corroborated by own knowledge?								

© JOHN MURRAY

GCSE Modern World History

The Learning Routes Model

The principles outlined above might be most readily grasped through models. The traditional model for meeting the different needs of pupils can be visualised as follows:

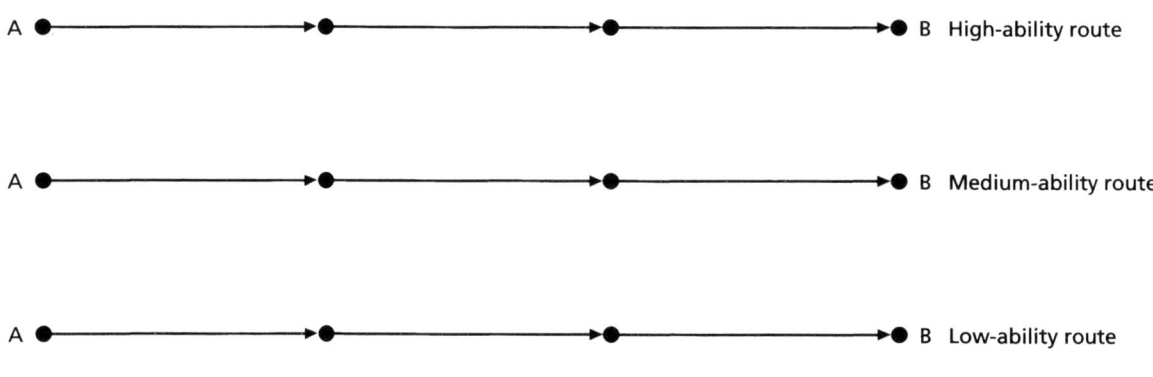

A ●————————→●————————→●————————→● B High-ability route

A ●————————→●————————→●————————→● B Medium-ability route

A ●————————→●————————→●————————→● B Low-ability route

● represents an important point in the Scheme of Work, such as a major task or piece of homework.

There are several difficulties with this model. The workload involved in administering different materials, particularly within a mixed-ability class, is extremely daunting. Also, there is the danger of the self-fulfilling prophecy, in which pupils relegated to the lower echelons perform to the expectations set. Finally, such a model has implications for progression. If each route indicates a discrete route, what of the pupil who is over-stretched or under-challenged?

This book attempts to make practical a slightly different model. Pupils follow the same route – the Focus Tasks. Teachers clearly need to make decisions about the detail of this. However, the differentiation in this model is based not on the content studied or the task but on the support mechanisms provided.

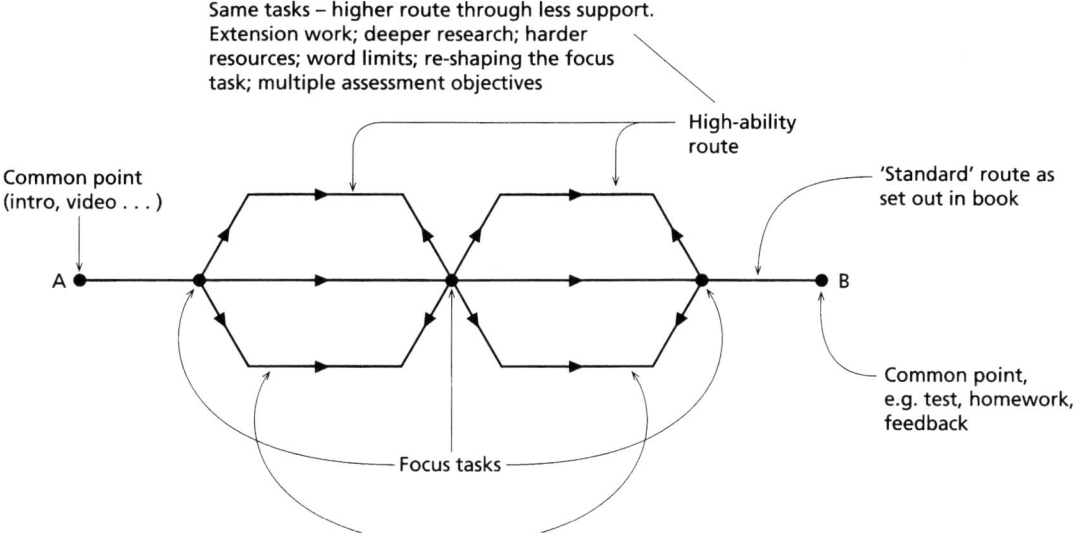

Same tasks – higher route through less support. Extension work; deeper research; harder resources; word limits; re-shaping the focus task; multiple assessment objectives

High-ability route

Common point (intro, video . . .)

'Standard' route as set out in book

A

B

Common point, e.g. test, homework, feedback

Focus tasks

Lower-ability route – pupils do same task but take this route via extra or simpler resources. Recording and writing frames; simpler presentation formats; word limits; narrower research

How to use the worksheets

Aim

Resources section for teachers or pupils to note where relevant information can be found

Space in margin – teacher can write specific instructions or advice for specific pupils

Some worksheets might be more cost effective as OHT masters

Ideas for extension work

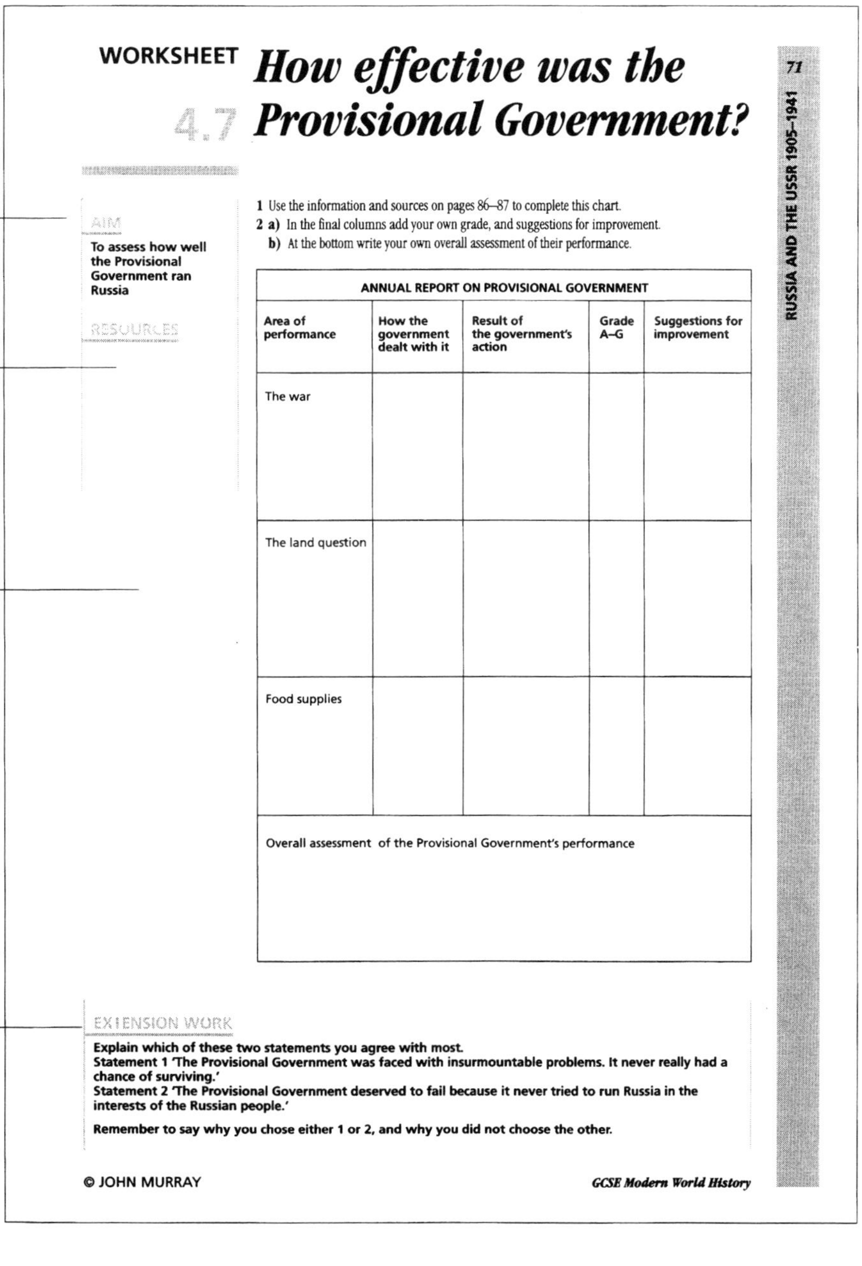

WORKSHEET

4.7 *How effective was the Provisional Government?*

71

RUSSIA AND THE USSR 1905–1941

AIM

To assess how well the Provisional Government ran Russia

RESOURCES

1 Use the information and sources on pages 86–87 to complete this chart.
2 a) In the final columns add your own grade, and suggestions for improvement.
   b) At the bottom write your own overall assessment of their performance.

ANNUAL REPORT ON PROVISIONAL GOVERNMENT				
Area of performance	How the government dealt with it	Result of the government's action	Grade A–G	Suggestions for improvement
The war				
The land question				
Food supplies				
Overall assessment of the Provisional Government's performance				

EXTENSION WORK

Explain which of these two statements you agree with most.
Statement 1 'The Provisional Government was faced with insurmountable problems. It never really had a chance of surviving.'
Statement 2 'The Provisional Government deserved to fail because it never tried to run Russia in the interests of the Russian people.'
Remember to say why you chose either 1 or 2, and why you did not choose the other.

© JOHN MURRAY

GCSE Modern World History

The structure of the Pupil's Book

Questions

Clear headings

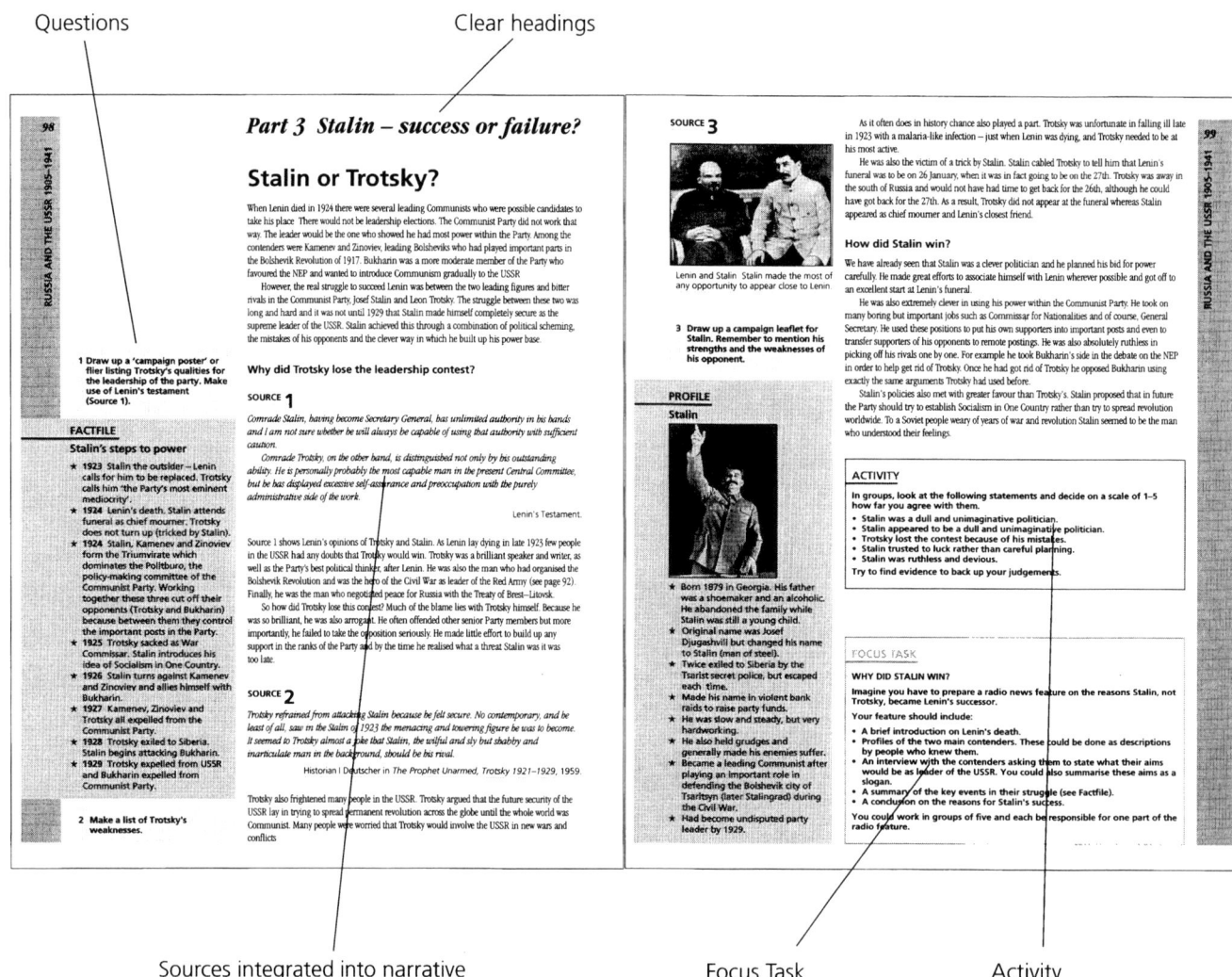

Sources integrated into narrative

Focus Task

Activity

The chapters

The book is designed for the major Modern World History syllabuses. The content has been divided into chapters which strike a balance between the sometimes rigid definitions set out by examination boards and the need to present pupils with a story which makes sense.

Teachers will have little difficulty in recognising the elements of the book peculiar to the core content of their particular syllabus. However, they should not feel restricted to that part of the syllabus. As is described below, all of the chapters are built upon Focus Tasks which identify and set pupils the task of showing their understanding of a key issue. There will be many instances where a teacher may find it profitable to ask pupils to tackle a Focus Task from a chapter which is optional in their particular course because it will add to the depth and/or the breadth of their understanding. For example, in order to give a rounded picture to pupils studying the Vietnam War, you may want to ask them to attempt the Focus Task on China's foreign relations (page 283), even though they are not formally studying the topic. Similarly, pupils not studying the Great War as an option topic could gain much from looking at selected Focus Tasks from Chapter 2 as background to the Versailles Treaty, the League of Nations and Appeasement. Even if pupils are not studying Chapter 5 on Germany between the wars, there are numerous aspects of Hitler's ideas and policies which must be regarded as essential background to the origins of the Second World War.

The Focus Statement

All chapters begin with a short Focus Statement. All topics in Modern World History are challenging and many of the chapters in the book go into topics in some depth. With this in mind, the Focus Statement acts as an 'advance reminder' to pupils about what they will cover in the rest of the chapter. In most chapters this Focus Statement is accompanied by a timeline of the events to be covered in the chapter.

Research shows that pupils are much more confident and organised in their work, and indeed spend a greater proportion of their time on the task, if they have this overall snapshot of the topic.

The Issue Starter

The book tries to introduce each chapter by going straight to the heart of the material being studied. Sometimes this simply means starting at the chronological beginning. However, to truly get 'history in focus' it is often necessary to start at the end or in the middle of a topic. In this way the really big issues which put topics into their historical context are raised early on. Also, pupils get to see the human side of events. This can sometimes be lost in Modern World History, even though it is a vital factor in pupils gaining a proper understanding of the topics they are studying. For example, beginning the chapter on the League of Nations with the cliff-hanging debate in Congress over the Treaty of Versailles has certain advantages over starting the topic with the Covenant of the League.

Headings, sources and text

In keeping with the philosophy already outlined, the headings have an important function in guiding pupils through each chapter. As well as indicating content areas and themes, the headings aim to alert pupils to important issues, key points and areas of debate or controversy. Pupils are regularly asked to gather their thoughts and to demonstrate their understanding of sections studied through Focus Tasks which come at the end of most sections (see below).

The text itself aims to provide a clear, driving story, to inform pupils but also to carry them along with a sense of the period. Topics are covered in some depth, and in keeping with the new guidelines for GCSE courses, the narrative is closely tied to the source materials so that each can provide a context for the other. To help pupils to get a feel for how history should be written, assertions are supported at all times either by relevant factual evidence or by reference to source material which may be primary or secondary, visual or written, statistical or graphical. There is a strong emphasis on visual sources, again to stimulate interest but also to support weaker pupils and to provide all pupils with images of the people and events they are studying quite literally to help pupils get 'history in focus'.

Pupil tasks

Pupil activities in the book are divided into three types.

Questions

The marginal questions, in coloured boxes, are designed to support pupils as they read through the text and look at the sources. They draw pupils' attention to important points or subtle messages within sources which might be missed without careful and thorough reading. Pupils can write answers in their exercise books in order to build up a bank of useful notes and information. However, the questions are challenging questions. This means that they require thought and care from pupils if they are to be answered effectively. These questions are not simply about copying large chunks of text from the textbook into the exercise book.

Many of the questions could be used as starting points for class discussions. Indeed, in most cases the recommendation in this Teacher's Resource Book is that these questions be used in such a way.

Activities

As well as questions there are activities (outlined in red). These are on the whole more creative exercises which ask pupils to use the information and evidence which they have collected and apply it in some context which asks them to show their understanding of a topic or issue. Thus by asking pupils to draw up campaign posters for or against the Nazis in the 1930s you are challenging them to demonstrate their knowledge. However, they are also challenged to show their understanding of the factors which concerned Germans at that time, and the methods and ideas which would have appealed to these people. Most of the activities are suitable for pupils working in pairs or groups to help and support each other by sharing and comparing their ideas. In some cases extra worksheet support is provided in this Teacher's Resource Book.

Focus Tasks

The Focus Tasks could be seen as the building blocks of the chapters. Like the questions and the activities, their emphasis is on pupils showing their understanding. However, their aim is also to pull together the information, evidence and ideas which pupils will have gathered in particular sections within a chapter so that they can develop and demonstrate an overall understanding of events, issues, historical controversies and context. The Focus Tasks can therefore be used as reference points around which to plan schemes of work for a GCSE syllabus. This Teacher's Resource Book contains a worksheet to support the most important Focus Tasks in the book, and to provide effective strategies for differentiation (see pages 3–7).

Revision and the GCSE examination

The Pupil's Book, and therefore this Teacher's Resource Book as well, are designed to help pupils and teachers with any Modern World History course at this level. However, the book has taken as its organising structure the MEG Modern World History syllabus, which is centred around key questions and focus points. Clearly these will heavily influence the nature and structure of the final examinations for this board. It should be stressed, however, that some key questions and focus points are an equally valid way of approaching the requirements of other syllabuses.

With this in mind the teacher must be doubly aware of the significance of the Focus Tasks. As stated earlier in this introduction, they act as rallying points at which pupils can bring together and assess their own knowledge and understanding, and the progress they have made. However, they also have a greater significance in terms of preparing pupils for examinations. The Focus Tasks target focus points and key questions in the MEG syllabus. As such, they are designed to focus pupils' minds on important aspects of the content of the course and to develop their understanding of that content. They are also designed to produce substantial pieces of work in the process. The Focus Tasks will therefore promote quality learning on the 'first pass' at a content area of the syllabus, but also provide pupils with a solid piece of work which will serve them well as a revision aid in the future.

To further complement this process, a number of revision guides for GCSE History are also available (see page ii). Aimed at pupils rather than at teachers, these books encourage pupils to actively take control of their own revision. They also provide revision sessions, in which past examination questions are taken apart and the aims of the examiner are discussed. The overall effect is that pupils know the parameters within which they are working. The revision guides for the new syllabuses will be available in early 1998.

History and technology

Clearly as a core textbook the Pupil's Book aims to provide a comprehensive resource, adequate to cover an entire Modern World Syllabus. There are few teachers who will use only one resource in working through a GCSE examination course. With this in mind we have tried, through the Focus Tasks and through the worksheets and frameworks for recording and writing, to provide a central core resource which can be complemented by other resources. The History teacher needs to be aware of the increasing variety of resources and opportunities offered by video and audio technology, but above all by the rapidly developing possibilities offered by Information Technology in the form of computers.

In 1995 the Historical Association, in conjunction with NCET, began a History and IT Support Project. The aim of the Project was to promote and disseminate good practice and high-quality materials in which high-level History is achieved through the use of IT. As a result of this project, and of much imaginative work in LEAs and from software developers, the historian is presented with increasingly powerful tools to aid pupils' learning in History. Internet and e-mail allow access to the resources of the world's archives. CD-ROMs offer vast amounts of information, again with very simple access. Expert systems, which analyse and respond to pupils' answers to (relatively straightforward) questions, can give pupils the instant attention they want. They also provide the potential for really exciting home study revision tools.

IT can also help with the more routine tasks. For example, many teachers (including the author), have experimented with putting the writing frames and recording formats much used in this Teacher's Resource Book on to templates on a word processor or DTP package. On a word processor, pupils can draft and redraft their answer as many times as they wish. They can even save each attempt to answer a question, ask for feedback from the teacher and then look back at their own progress. In some of the causal link diagrams, the computer makes it a simple job to enlarge, reduce and link cause boxes.

The relationship between The Twentieth-Century World at KS3 and GCSE Modern World History

All teachers are now faced with the problem that, whatever the GCSE course they follow, there is almost certain to be a degree of overlap between what pupils cover at KS3 and in their GCSE courses. This is a particularly relevant issue to teachers of Modern World History, since the majority of pupils will enter Y10 having studied The Twentieth-Century World at the end of Y9. The challenge for teachers and History departments is how to tackle this issue of overlap through their planning processes. In short, teachers must either try to avoid overlap, or they must use overlap constructively. Either way it is vital to face the issue of overlap head on and to develop a policy to deal with it.

Avoiding overlap makes sense in certain circumstances. For example, it would not appear logical to conduct a depth study on Nazi Germany, and then to repeat the process as one of the optional topics in the GCSE course the following year.

However, avoiding overlap may not be the most profitable policy in planning pupils' progression from KS3 to GCSE. Careful planning and structuring of courses could allow the overlap to be constructive rather than simply repetitive.

• The overviews required by KS3 study units are potentially of great value in a GCSE course. For instance, pupils might complete their study of History in Y9 with display work which results in a chronology of the twentieth century. Such a chronology could be organised purely by date or might be further structured thematically – by geography, warfare, technology, human rights, etc. Pupils returning to Y10 might find their display work from the end of Y9 both stimulating and useful.

• In Y9 pupils look in overview at a new kind of warfare – trench warfare. In Y10/11 they get the chance to revisit this, and look at a wider range of source material to build on their Y9 work. This could involve coursework based on a field trip to the First World War battlefields. More able pupils can move on more swiftly, and progress to such issues as how trenches were represented, responsibility for the conditions faced, how they were endured, etc.

One overview aspect of the Y9 unit which causes problems is 'the legacy of the Second World War'. This can be more creatively handled if it is seen as the framing device for later work in Y10 and Y11 on the origins of the Cold War, and of superpower rivalry.

Planned content overlap might help still more in the case of low-ability pupils. One of the greatest problems for such pupils is the culture of 'one pass' learning which examination demands create. Pupils, regardless of ability, aptitude or maturity are given only one chance to understand complex content and concepts before the relentless tide of the course sweeps them on. Teachers might deliberately plan to cover the same material twice with a view to reinforcing really important content, concepts or ideas.

Constructive use of overlap might help weaker pupils understand, for example, the significance of the Treaty of Versailles, or the idea of Appeasement. These seminal topics from Y9 could be revisited in Y10 for weaker pupils, and also, for the more able, used as the basis for exploring intrepretations and historiography.

• Overlap can also help weaker pupils with History methods and skills. As one of their depth studies in Y9, pupils can be introduced to a type of investigation, for example the study of the role of an individual which can stand them in better stead for such studies in Y10/11. Some pupils could even benefit from studying the same individual again, but in greater depth.

An important new study of how the Twentieth-Century World unit fits into the KS3 and KS4 curriculum as a whole has been written by Christine Counsell and published by the Historical Association (1997).

SECTION 1: **THE FIRST WORLD WAR**

The causes of the First World War
Who should bear the blame?

Key features of the chapter

	Issue covered	Assessment elements	Format(s) for pupil work
Focus Task (p.8): The Alliances	Concerns of major states, causes of tension	Historical knowledge, key features of historical situation	Research, recording table, written work (including extended)
Activity (p.12): The spark which lit the bonfire	Causal factors	Deploying knowledge	Discussion, visual representation, extended writing
Focus Task (p.13): Was Germany to blame for the war?	Responsibility for the war?	Sources, interpretations	Discussion, presentation, extended writing

Murder in Sarajevo – the Issue Starter

In this instance there can be few better ways to get to the heart of the topic than to consider the human tragedy which set the wheels in motion. Using the Focus Statement, teachers can quickly establish that Europe was a tense place in 1914. The scene then switches to Sarajevo, where the fate of these great empires and states lies in the hands of a group of young men.

Make sure pupils are aware who Franz Ferdinand was – the Archduke of Austria, whose empire covered much of central and eastern Europe. A modern parallel might be a visit by a US president to the Middle East. Imagine the security which would surround such a visit. Using **Source 1A** (probably best read aloud) pupils could first of all try to empathise with Princip and his fellow gang members:

1 Why are these teenagers waiting to commit murder?
2 How do you think they feel, armed with guns and bombs and planning to poison themselves if they are caught?
3 Are these young men the same sort of people who have been responsible for acts of terrorism in Northern Ireland or Palestine?

Then they could turn to the victims using **Sources 1A** and **2**:

1 Does Source 2 help you to form any impression of what the Archduke and his wife were like?
2 After reading Source 1B, do pupils have any sympathy for the victims?

3 Does their view change when they think about why the young Serbs attacked them in the first place?

Finally, using **questions 1** and **2** on **page 4** it might be interesting to speculate on how events could have turned out differently. These questions could be revisited at different stages in the topic as a complete picture builds up of the international scene by 1914.

The Alliances

This is a long and fairly detailed section, but it is necessary if pupils are to understand the situation in Europe in 1914. It could also be extremely useful as a background study which helps to explain the thinking of political leaders in the 1920s and 1930s. There is also scope for mentioning the modern descendants of the armed camps (most notably NATO), making the point that politicians still believe today that the most effective way of preserving peace is a strong armed force. This could be a useful device in turning the focus of study away from 'How could they do it?' to 'How did it happen?'.

There are many ways of using this section. **Worksheet 1.1** contains an enlarged version of the table in the **Focus Task** on **page 8**. It is advisable for pupils to look at this before they read the text, in order to give them a clear purpose for their reading. Part 3 is clearly a subjective question but the rating scale helps them to gain a sense of priority and perspective. Part 4 essentially asks pupils to apply the knowledge they have just gleaned from the worksheet exercise. Some prompts are included to help them recognise the types of problems and the countries where they occur.

Worksheet 1.2 provides an alternative (albeit similar) activity which asks pupils to look at each of the states in the alliances more from their own perspective than for their role in international affairs.

Questions 1 and 2 on pages 6–7 could work well as discussion questions or as written exercises. In the latter case it would probably be useful to provide pupils with a checklist of features to look for when considering the motives of states. Such a list might include:

- Relations with neighbours
- Relations with states in own and opposing alliances
- Ambitions — territorial, imperial/colonial
- Military programmes
- Major concerns.

Questions 1 and 2 on page 8 follow on logically from the work on pages 6–7. They also provide valuable practice in translating sometimes opaque collections of figures into hard political and military considerations. After carrying out the exercise it might be worthwhile for pupils to put themselves in the position of the wavering Italians. Now they have had a good look at the figures do they still want to be part of the Triple Alliance?

Questions 3 and 4 try to bring together the main points and issues of this section through the medium of the American cartoon, **Source 9**. Question 3 simply asks pupils to turn into words the message of the cartoon. Their findings from the Focus Task should then enable them to tackle question 4, which essentially asks them to state whether or not they agree with the rather pessimistic view of the cartoon. This question could be used as the basis for a piece of extended writing. Weaker students might find the writing frame on **Worksheet 1.3** helpful in structuring their answers.

The tension builds, 1900–1914

This part of the chapter plays an important role in establishing the processes which led to the outbreak of war. However, armament and disarmament are key themes in the history of the whole of the twentieth century.

Worksheet 1.4 provides a map which will help pupils with **questions 5–7** on **page 9**. The map will help to give a visual clue to Britain's uneasiness about the German fleet. These questions also provide a sharpening exercise for the source-based investigation on **Worksheet 1.5**, which addresses the arms race as a whole. The aim of the investigation is for pupils to look at the various sources in the chapter relevant to this issue and to practise skills of evaluation and cross-referencing. At the same time, the accompanying text should provide a helpful context for the sources. Ideally, pupils will find this contextual information useful, and at the same time will see the need for all evidence to be viewed in context, a key feature of innumerable examiners' reports on GCSE examinations.

The Activity on page 12 is intended to be flexible so that all or part of it can be tackled in small-group or whole-class discussion, or as individual written work. A pupil copy of the bonfire diagram is provided on **Worksheet 1.6**, with plenty of space around the graphic for pupils to jot notes or add labels if the logs are too small for their handwriting! The second part of the exercise is addressing a key issue in historical causation. The worksheet provides prompts and a skeleton timeline to help pupils see why the bonfire went up in 1914 rather than in 1905.

Did Germany cause the war?

The first source of this section, **Source 20**, is the first of several extracts from *The Great War – The Standard History of the All-Europe Conflict*. It is worth pointing out to pupils the patriotism of this publication, and the extent to which it was wartime propaganda.

The section is in the form of a series of sources marshalled around a **Focus Task** and taking the form of a trial. The preparatory phases are probably best run in small groups. Indeed the entire trial could be run in this way with the groups then reporting their separate verdicts back to the class. The whole class could then debate the issue.

Worksheet 1.7 provides a framework for this exercise.

WORKSHEET

The Alliances

1.1

AIM

To describe and explain why there was tension between the major powers in 1914

RESOURCES

1 Look at the chart below and then read pages 5–7.

	Germany	Austria–Hungary	Italy
Britain			
France			
Russia			

2 Using the descriptions of each country fill out the chart to show causes of tension between them. You may not have to fill out all the spaces. Also use one or two words to show the cause of any tension.

3 You are now going to try to decide which relationship is the greatest source of tension. It might help you to use a scale of 1 to 5. A rating of 1 means that there are no major sources of tension between the states, but a 5 means things are very serious.

4 Explain how the following contributed to tensions between the European powers:

a) Colonies (see section on Germany)

b) People wanting independence (see section on Austria–Hungary)

c) Arms build-up (see section on Russia)

WORKSHEET

1.2

The Alliances

AIM

To identify the key features of the Alliances in 1914 and their relative strengths

RESOURCES

Read through the information and sources on pages 5–7. Use what you find out to complete the table below.

	Main concerns	Plans and ambitions	Industrial strength	Military strength	Comments
Central Powers/Triple Alliance					
Triple Entente					

Do you think that the Alliances made war more likely or less likely?

AIM

To use a range of source materials and examples to support a balanced argument

RESOURCES

The arguments to support the view that the Alliances made war more likely are:

* _____
* _____
* _____
* _____

The arguments to support the view that the Alliances made war less likely are:

* _____
* _____
* _____
* _____

On considering the evidence, my conclusion is that

_____

_____

_____

_____

I believe this because

* _____
* _____
* _____
* _____

WORKSHEET *The naval arms race*

1.4

GCSE Modern World History

AIM

To use source material to explain why there was rivalry between Germany and Britain

RESOURCES

Key

British Empire

The extent of the British Empire in 1914

1 Look at Source 13 on page 9 and the map above. Explain why Britain was concerned by Germany's naval plans.

_____

_____

_____

_____

2 How did Germany react to Britain's concerns (look at Source 11)?

_____

_____

_____

_____

3 Do you think that either country was acting unreasonably? Give your reasons.

_____

_____

_____

_____

_____

_____

_____

WORKSHEET

1.5

The arms race before 1914 – source investigation

AIM

To use and evaluate a range of source materials to investigate the importance of the arms build-up in Europe up to 1914

RESOURCES

Look carefully at Sources 14–18.

1 Read Source 15.
  a) What is meant by the term 'arms race'?
  b) Give one example of this type of rivalry which was taking place in Europe before 1914.

2 Look at Source 14.
  How useful is this sort of information to a historian studying the arms race?

3 Read Source 17.
  How reliable is this source as evidence for German attitudes towards the arms race before the First World War?

4 Look at Sources 15 and 18.
  Which of these two sources would you regard as being of greater value to a historian studying the Arms Race?

5 Look at Sources 14–18.
  'Germany was responsible for the arms race and therefore for causing the First World War.' Do the sources support this view?

Use the table below to help you to organise your thoughts.

Source	14	15	16	17	18
Contains relevant information?					
Supports the view?					
Reliable source (Reasons)	⁄				
Supported by own knowledge? (Examples)					
Supported by other sources in selection? (Explain)					

WORKSHEET

1.6

Long- and short-term causes of the First World War

AIM

To describe and explain the different types of causes which contributed to the outbreak of war in 1914

RESOURCES

1 The atmosphere in Europe between 1900 and 1914 has been compared to a bonfire waiting to be lit. On the diagram below, add labels to suggest factors which made war possible.

Put major factors on big sticks, less important factors on smaller sticks.

Add more sticks to the fire if you wish to add more factors.

2 From 1900 to 1914 there was a series of crises and disputes among the European powers:

1900   Colonial rivalries between Britain, France and Germany

1905   Moroccan crisis
France tries to take control of Morocco. Germany protests but loses argument as France, Britain and Russia stick together

1908   Bosnian crisis
Austria–Hungary takes full control of Bosnia–Herzegovina. (There are many Serbs in this region.) Russia and Serbia protest but Austria succeeds

1911   Second Moroccan crisis
Another dispute between Germany and France over Morocco, with similar results

1912–13   Balkan Wars
A series of wars involving the Balkan states and Turkey. The most important result was that Serbia emerged as the leading Balkan state and was a potential enemy on Austria's border

Why do you think the Sarajevo murder 'lit the fire' when these previous events had not? Mention these points in your answer:
- Austria's worries about Serbia by 1914 (see pages 4–6)
- How international problems had built up on top of each other to increase tension (see pages 4–8)
- How the arms race increased tensions (see pages 8–11)
- The way the alliances worked in 1914 (see page 5)

WORKSHEET

Was Germany to blame for the war?

1.7

AIM

To use a range of sources to compare different interpretations of the outbreak of war

RESOURCES

Your task is to look over the evidence and hold a re-trial, looking back from today. You will study evidence and hear from witnesses. You must then reach one of these four verdicts:

Verdict 1 Germany was rightly blamed for starting the war.
Verdict 2 Germany was mainly responsible for starting the war but the other powers should accept some of the blame.
Verdict 3 All of the major powers helped start the war. They should share the blame.
Verdict 4 No-one was to blame. The powers were swept along towards an inevitable war. It could not be stopped.

The table will help you as you examine the evidence presented by the witnesses.

Witness	1	2	3	4	5	6	7	8
Witness (Who?)								
Which verdict?								
What evidence?								
Can I trust the witness? Date and origin? Involved? Valuable? Reliable?								
Corroborated (backed up) by other sources?								
Corroborated by own knowledge?								

Summary

The findings of the Court are that Verdict _____ is the correct verdict.

The evidence to support Verdict 1 is

- _____

- _____

The evidence to support Verdict 2 is

- _____

- _____

The evidence to support Verdict 3 is

- _____

- _____

The evidence to support Verdict 4 is

- _____

- _____

The evidence, on balance, therefore supports Verdict _____ because

- _____

- _____

- _____

- _____

- _____

Britain and the First World War: 1914–1918

2

Key features of the chapter

	Issue covered	Assessment elements	Format(s) for pupil work
Activity (p. 16): Reactions to war	Comparison of different responses to war in 1914	Key features of historical situation	Newspaper report on reactions across Europe
Focus Task (p. 21): Christmas 1914	Why the war was not over by December 1914	Selecting and deploying information	Two reports – public and politicians' view
Focus Task (p. 22): The trenches	How trench warfare was organised	Use of sources	Annotated diagram, commentary on evidence
Focus Task (p. 27): The Western Front	How did the fighting on the Western Front change?	Use of sources, selecting and deploying information	Structured extended writing
Activity (p. 30): Turning points	What were the turning points on the Western Front?	Describing and analysing events and changes	Research and presentation of case for turning points
Focus Task (p. 30): Stalemate	How was the stalemate broken?	Selecting and deploying information	Supported research and structured writing
Focus Task (p. 32): Conditions for soldiers	What was life like on the Western Front?	Use of sources, key features of an historical situation	Reconstructed diaries or commentaries on diaries
Focus Task (p. 34): Control of information	How was the war portrayed?	Use of sources	Supported research, commentary on sources
Focus Task (p. 35): The other fronts	Comparative timeline of events on other fronts	Describing and analysing events and changes	Annotated timeline
Focus Task (p. 37): Gallipoli	Why did the Gallipoli campaign fail?	Use of sources, describing and analysing events	Research and structured report
Focus Task (p. 40): The Eastern Front	How important was Russia's role in the war?	Selecting and deploying information, describing and analysing events	Choosing between opinions
Focus Task (p. 41): Different fronts in World War I	The main developments on each front	Describing events	Comparative timeline
Focus Task (p. 45): New warfare	Links between war in air, on land and sea	Key features of historical situation	Annotated diagram
Activity/Factfile (p. 47): The Home Front	How was Britain organised to fight the war?	Use of sources, key features of historical situation	Commentary on sources
Focus Task (p. 53): Propaganda	How was propaganda used by the government?	Selecting and deploying information, describing and analysing events	Structured report on aims and use of propaganda
Focus Task (p. 54): Support for the war	How consistent was support for the war?	Selecting and deploying information, key features of historical situation	Structured extended writing
Focus Task (p. 57): Women at war	What was the impact of the war on women?	Use of sources, selecting and deploying information, key features of historical situation	Structured research and presentation

Part 1 BREAKING THE STALEMATE ON THE WESTERN FRONT

The mood in 1914 – the Issue Starter

This focus on the transformation wrought by the war begins with an examination of the young men who were called up (or volunteered) and went off enthusiastically to war in 1914. Pupils could be asked to read Sources 2–8 and describe the mood of 1914.

Important points for them to consider would be:

1 Do they have brothers of the right age for military service?
2 How would they have felt about seeing them go off to war?
3 Why does there seem to have been such enthusiasm?
4 Would a war today be greeted with this enthusiasm?
5 Was there really such enthusiasm? Is it possible that there were protests or doubts, and if so why do we know so little about them?

These questions would form ideal preparation for the **Activity** on **page 16**. As well as, or perhaps as an alternative to the article, pupils could run a short report for an imaginary TV or radio news programme of 1914. Roving reporters could interview the soldiers, their officers, and civilians in the crowd as the soldiers embark for France.

The war on the Western Front reaches stalemate

The aim of this section is to highlight the extent to which the soldiers, politicians and military commanders were unprepared for the type of war which was to develop. This then enables pupils to grasp why the war developed into a stalemate which was not expected and for which in the early stages the participants were not prepared and not appropriately equipped.

Question 1 on page 17 is a straightforward source comprehension exercise, suitable for a written answer or analysis using the formula outlined on **Worksheet 3.2** in the next chapter. However, it could also be the basis for a fruitful discussion and the teasing out of the context of the source. The cartoon shows the obvious David and Goliath scenario but it also speaks volumes about the British perspective. The Kaiser is aged but nonetheless formidable. The cartoon contains an unspoken appeal to the British government to help Belgium. Teachers could discuss this with pupils and point out Britain's responsibilities in the Treaty of London. Pupils could work out that the cartoon is urging the British government to honour its commitment to Belgium.

Questions 1 and 2 on page 18 further reinforce the idea of the strangeness and shock of this new war. They would be well suited to written work. Pupils could be encouraged to think of Walter Bloem as one of the young men whose experiences they considered in the opening section and in the activity on the mood of 1914.

The sections on the Marne and the first Battle of Ypres also raise the issue of the experiences of the commanders as well as those of the soldiers. Pupils need to appreciate also that as the war showed few signs of ending politicians and people began to demand news, preferably news of victories. This is the basis of the **Focus Task** on **page 21**. This has two main aims:

* For pupils to show their understanding of the text and sources in this section by explaining in full and frank terms why the war reached a stalemate.
* For pupils to use their findings to show their understanding of the political realities of the situation which military leaders found themselves in. The creation of a selective picture for the public back home requires quite sophisticated thinking. **Worksheet 2.1** will help pupils to organise their ideas.

What was the fighting like on the Western Front?

Question 1 on page 23 again attempts to bring the human aspect of the war to the fore of pupils' minds. The question would work equally well as a written or discussion exercise. It may be helpful for some pupils to be given a series of prompts to use as headings to compile and organise their lists. Teachers can judge the amount of guidance their own pupils will need. Such a list might contain the following headings:

Combat equipment
- Personal – e.g. rifle, bullets, bayonet, grenades
- Non-personal – e.g. shells, artillery pieces, mortars

Support equipment
- Transport – e.g. motor or horse vehicles
- Trench defences – e.g. barbed wire, sandbags
- Personal – rations, replacement uniforms, field dressings, trenching tools.

Worksheet 2.2 is designed to support pupils tackling the **Focus Task** on **page 22** and the questions on **page 23**. Pupils may be asked to draw their own diagram or to label their own photocopied version provided in the worksheet. The question contains prompts as to where pupils can look for the required information.

The key skill being developed here is the use, as opposed to transference, of information contained in primary sources. By labelling the diagram pupils are showing their understanding of the numerous written accounts of the trenches contained in the body of the text. Pupils might find it helpful to know that the white patches in Source 19 show chalk. The topsoil has been blasted away. They are exercising the same skills in **questions 2 and 3**.

Worksheet 2.3 aims to support pupils with the final two questions. They can use the evaluation grid to assess the special characteristics of each of the different types of evidence (**question 2**). Teachers may wish to ask their pupils to tackle **question 3** without support. Alternatively, pupils can use the supplied hypothesis to guide them as they decide why there are such discrepancies between the trenches shown in **Source 20**.

Finally, the extension exercise offers pupils the opportunity either to broaden their search into source materials to produce the briefing leaflet, or to practise examination-type questions. Teachers may wish to limit pupils to other sources in the book in their search, or there may be opportunities to search IT or visual sources. For option (**b**), a writing framework is provided to help less confident pupils to organise their answers.

The aim of the questions on **page 26** is similar to that in the preceding Focus Task. As well as comprehending **Source 27**, pupils need to show that they have a grasp of the context of the events described. They will find that the source and the questions become straightforward if they read the text on machine guns and the source together.

The Focus Task on page 27 aims to pull all of the points and issues in the section together. Pupils might find Task A more stimulating if they have to create actual training manuals as they might have appeared at the respective times. **Worksheet 2.4** supports this Focus Task.

Task B asks pupils to show their understanding of all of the material that they have covered so far – to use information as well as simply move it around. A structure for the paragraphs is provided in the task, but weaker pupils may find the following reference points valuable.

Paragraph 1 – how war was different from what was expected –
- Mood in 1914, pages 15–16
- Why trench warfare developed, pages 22–23
- Walter Bloem's and Billy Congreve's experiences, pages 18 and 20.

Paragraph 2 – techniques and equipment –
- Trenches
- Artillery
(Look back at the answer to question 1 on page 23.)

Paragraph 3 – continuity as opposed to change –
• Tactics
• Importance of supplies and transport
• Methods of communication

Breaking the stalemate

This is a key section of the chapter and the subject is thus covered in some depth, but with the emphasis more on narrative than on source evaluation. Nevertheless, there are several important and rewarding questions which can be studied.

The Activity on page 30 tries to establish an overview in pupils' minds of the causal factors which began to change the course of the war between 1916 and 1918. The Activity is well suited to group discussion followed by a teacher-led class debriefing. As indicated in **Worksheet 2.4**, the activity could then be supported by follow-up work in the following Focus Task in which pupils make judgements about the relative importance of causes.

Some pupils may need help in thinking about the key events of each year. The following list may be useful, if teachers feel that their pupils need extra guidance.

1916 – Battle of Verdun, Somme (tactics and consequences)
1917 – USA enters war, Russian Revolution, effects of blockade on Germany
1918 – Ludendorff shows how stalemate can be broken, Allied counter attack.

Pupils could use the reports of the other groups (and their own work) to draw up a diagram to summarise the importance of these three years. **Worksheet 2.4** contains a starter framework which pupils could copy, extend and adapt. The key point is that they should be able to 'justify their lines of connection'.

This Activity therefore acts as ideal preparation for the **Focus Task** which follows it and which attempts to pull together the greater part of the material studied so far. **Worksheet 2.5** provides the framework to carry out parts 1–3 of the task.

Part 4 is extension work. Pupils can use their findings from parts 1–3 to complete the first section on why the stalemate occurred. Pupils' diagrams from the Activity above can be used as the framework for explaining how and why the stalemate was eventually broken. By indicating what the key events were in 1916–18 and explaining how they were connected ('justifying their lines'), pupils can show a true understanding of the forces which brought the war to a close.

What was life like in the trenches?

This section covers the aspect of the war which pupils arguably find more fascinating than any other. Because of the wealth of high-quality material available, the tasks and activities focus on the handling and interpretation of source material. Teachers and indeed pupils may well be able to complement the sources in this section with local materials relevant to the topic.

Sources 34–41 all build up to the **Focus Task** on **page 32**. Perhaps the most effective form of preparation would be to read through this section and the sources with the class, to get across the true atmosphere, both positive and negative, of the trenches. The Bairnsfather cartoons (Sources 34 and 46) are a good starting point – pupils could see the humour there and possibly suggest the sort of accent with which Bill might speak. As they look at Sources 37–41, the accents idea could be used to get pupils to think about the type of person who is the author of each source. Pupils will need to read the source and look at its provenance carefully before they decide what kind of accent the writer would have!

The thinking which goes into this preparation should then equip pupils to launch into the **Focus Task.** Pupils may feel confident enough to determine some of the parameters of the task themselves. The three entries could represent the same soldier at different times or in different moods. Equally, the entries could represent different ranks and even nationalities.

The questions on **pages 33 and 34** provide more opportunities to work with source material. They could be undertaken as written or discussion exercises, but the key point is to comprehend the meaning and intention of the sources and to explain this in a coherent fashion. The Bairnsfather cartoons are wonderfully atmospheric and are an ideal medium for small-group or whole-class discussion. The question on page 34 as to why some leaders were unhappy about the cartoons should throw up some interesting points.

The Activity on page 34 should prove relatively simple. The main point to emphasise is that different types of censorship were going on. As well as the official forms of censorship, to be looked at later in the chapter, there was the much more important self-censorship of the soldiers who wished to protect their families from the horrific experiences they had gone through. This is where the process of pupils editing their own diaries becomes especially relevant.

Worksheet 2.6 provides the framework for the **Focus Task** on **page 34**. The extension task on the worksheet will give pupils the opportunity to put their skills into practice in an examination-format question.

Part 2   THE WAR ON OTHER FRONTS

This section opens with an 'umbrella' focus task which is given more detail on **Worksheet 2.7**. There are several aims behind this task. The most obvious is the evaluation of the similarities and differences between the campaigns fought in different parts of the world. However, at least equally important is that by carrying out this comparison pupils are constantly reviewing the work they are currently doing and their recent work on the Western Front.

This is a powerful methodology for reinforcing knowledge in the form of active revision as pupils go along. It is also highly effective in pushing pupils to put their knowledge of one area into context by comparing it with another.

Gallipoli

The questions based on **Source 4** on **page 37** are probably best handled as written exercises, given that there is a clear emphasis on evaluation and comprehension of source material. Useful follow-up discussion could involve pupils reviewing what they have read about Gallipoli so far and comparing it with the Western Front. A look back at the poetry of Wilfred Owen and Sassoon (Sources 28 and 45 in Part 1) would pay dividends here. Pupils would then be in a good position to tackle the Focus Task at the beginning of Part 2, either before or after working on the Focus Task on Gallipoli.

The other questions on **page 37** might be best used as a discussion stimulus in preparation for the main Focus Task. **Question 5** will be particularly useful when pupils start to organise themselves to tackle the Focus Task.

The Focus Task on page 37 has the potential to be customised to the ability and needs of different pupils. **Worksheet 2.8** provides a framework for this. Teachers can differentiate the activity in a wide variety of ways:

• By asking pupils to focus on one or more issues (e.g. the quality of the leadership, the quality of the evidence)
• By advising on, restricting or extending the range of material which pupils are required to examine
• By allowing different formats for presenting conclusions (report, annotated diagram)
• By asking pupils to tackle both questions rather than just one.

In addition, a writing frame is provided to help pupils to structure their answers.

The Balkans and the Middle East

The aim of this section is above all to provide pupils with a narrative so that they gain a complete picture of the campaigns. There are no tasks dealing with the material in this section alone and therefore the Focus Task at the beginning becomes particularly important. It may prove worthwhile for pupils to read through this section with the teacher and then fill in the relevant parts of the framework set out in **Worksheet 2.7**.

The Eastern Front

As in the preceding section, it is assumed that the **Focus Task** on **page 35** will be to the fore of pupils' minds as they work through the text. The **Focus Task** on **page 40** is relatively straightforward but is worth tackling as a written exercise because of the importance of the question posed. **Worksheet 2.9** provides a writing frame to help pupils to organise their thinking for this task.

The war at sea

The purpose of this section is to complete pupils' picture of the war and to give them the final piece of the puzzle needed to complete the timeline in the **Focus Task** on **page 41**. An example timeline is provided in **Worksheet 2.10**. Follow-up work could ask pupils to discuss whether it is possible to say whether one theatre of conflict was more important than another. Perhaps more importantly, they can use the worksheet to show their understanding of the connections between different events at different times on the various fronts.

In addition, the development of new technology in the war at sea is explored in a comparative activity at the end of Part 2 (**page 45**).

The war in the air

Although in some ways the least important aspect of the war from a military point of view, the war in the air is highly significant. This feature of the fighting was a classic example of how the horrors of the reality of war allowed people to turn towards and exaggerate the importance of a method of combat that could to some degree still be seen as daring and noble.

This contrast could readily be explored with pupils by asking them to look at **questions 1–3** on **page 45** and read the sections on the war at sea and then the war in the air one after the other. Most will grasp that while sea power was much more important, it was much less exciting. The questions could form the basis of lively discussion in small groups, pairs or as a whole class.

Pupils should then be well prepared to tackle the **Focus Task** on **page 45**.

Part 3 THE HOME FRONT – HOW DID THE WAR AFFECT BRITAIN?

How was Britain organised to fight the war?

This part of the chapter looks back to one of the key points in the Focus Statement, namely the way in which the war changed Britain in terms of fundamental principles, ideas and accepted notions. The **Factfile** on **page 47** is designed as a reference tool for all of the activities in the section. There is a strong emphasis on using and evaluating source material in this section, and a key feature of successful work with sources is the provision of context.

Questions 1 and 2 on pages 48 and 49 are source-based exercises, well suited to written answers. Pupils may find it helpful to be reminded in brief of the features to consider when looking at visual sources, although a key exercise on cartoons is included in the next chapter of this book (page 50).

Background

- The date it was drawn – what else was going on at the same time?
- The country and the type of publication in which the poster was published.

Words

- Look at the caption (if the cartoon has one) – it is usually very blunt.

The poster itself

- Start by looking at the background if there is one – what kind of impression is it trying to give?
- Look at any figures and think about how the cartoonist has drawn them in terms of size, bulk and their position in relation to each other.
- Facial expressions are usually very important – they tell you whether the cartoonist thinks that a character is brave, cowardly, sincere, treacherous etc.

Pupils might benefit from a few helpful hints and prompts with question 2, such as:

1 Why was there such a need for men?
2 Why could some workers not be spared from their work?
3 Name one group of workers who felt that conscription would be just. Do they have a valid argument?
4 Name one group of workers who felt that conscription would not be just. Do they have a valid argument?

Some pupils might benefit from a writing frame:

The issue we are discussing is whether conscription in 1916 was fair.
The arguments put forward against conscription were:

- _____
- _____
- _____

The arguments put forward for conscription were:

- _____
- _____
- _____

DORA

The section on DORA is a key one in this part of the chapter as it provides the underlying information to support pupils as they investigate the extent to which Britain was truly mobilised for war. The questions on **page 50** are again suited to written answers and are asking pupils to use source material. However, it is important to stress that none of the questions can be tackled effectively unless pupils have read and understood the relevant section of the text and can therefore place the source in its appropriate context.

Questions 4–6 on page 51 might benefit from some preliminary briefing, but could be answered in discussion or in a written form. It is important for pupils to explain their answers, particularly as to why the government published Source 11 in the form it did (question 6).

The Focus Task on page 52 continues to emphasise the key themes of this section; pupils are asked to study the ways in which the war changed civilians' lives and are also asked to look at a seminal source in its context. **Worksheet 2.11** provides a copy of the source and space to answer parts 1–3 of the task. Part 4 demands that pupils have shown their understanding in the previous parts and now asks them to evaluate the source in the context of the information provided in the text and some of the other sources. Part 5 asks them to round off by suggesting how such an item as Source 12 is put together in the first place.

The Focus Task on page 53 builds on this understanding of how propaganda is created by asking pupils to look at selected pieces of propaganda and decide how well they meet certain objectives. Pupils could take this task further by extending the range of objectives and possibly testing other sources in this chapter.

This Focus Task complements the more structured **Activity** on the same page. The Activity will probably be most effective as a group exercise. The key aspect of it is that pupils draw up their propaganda rules and in doing so provide themselves with a tool they can use in the future. With this in mind it is important that the teacher should hold a class feedback session and ensure that pupils are armed with an effective tool!

Opposition to the war

This section continues to address the question of the impact of the war by looking at the attitudes of the British people towards it. The section charts the change from enthusiasm to a combination of grim determination and critical support for the government's handling of the war.

Questions 1 and 2 on page 54 require pupils to look very carefully at **Sources 14 and 15** and grasp their nuances. They may be better suited to discussion as the processes employed in the questions will be helpful in tackling the **Focus Task** for this section.

The essence of the task is to assess the mood of the British people at different stages of the war. For part 1 pupils should certainly refer to such issues as:

- Recruitment and conscription
- Munitions
- War work
- Food and rationing
- The media.

For part 2 they have a wide range of factors to choose from. Apart from those listed above they might wish to look at the effect of the Battle of the Somme on people at home or the role of newspapers or film.

Did the war change the role of women?

Most pupils will have studied the Home Front in the Second World War in Y9 and will have come across the opportunities that war brought to women. These opportunities were not so great in the First World War but the starting point of women in 1914 was such that in some respects the 1914–18 war brought greater changes.

Questions 3 and 4 on page 55 are fairly straightforward source-based questions, but they do introduce pupils to the concept that women shared fully in all aspects of war work. The resilience they showed was a revelation to many, and pupils can appreciate this through examining Asquith's change of heart in **questions 1–3** on **page 57**.

The Focus Task on page 57 attempts to bring all of this together by asking pupils to review the evidence and how far it supports three different hypotheses. **Worksheet 2.12** will help pupils to look at the evidence and produce a reasoned and structured conclusion.

WORKSHEET 2.1 *Why was the war not over by Christmas?*

AIM

To analyse and explain why the war was not over as expected by the end of 1914

RESOURCES

It is Christmas 1914. People were told that the war would be over by Christmas. You have to explain why it has not ended.

Work in pairs. You are going to write two reports about the progress of the war from August to December of 1914. One of you must write for the Prime Minister explaining events as fully as you can. The other must write for the general public back in Britain, with an encouraging message about how the war is going.

You may wish to mention these points:

- Successes and failures of the various plans
- The important battles which have taken place
- The new lessons being learnt about warfare
- The casualties
- The morale of the troops.

You should write a conclusion which includes:

- your own explanation of why the war was not over by Christmas
- your views on how the war will be fought through 1915.

When you have finished, compare your two reports:

- Are there differences in tone?
- Have you included different details?
- Is one more accurate than the other?

Planning

Before you write your answer look through the text and sources on pages 17–21. Then use the table below to make brief notes about the points in your report, including in each case the sources, sections or page numbers where you found relevant information. This will help you to organise your writing and ensure that you don't simply copy the text.

	Note down the points you want to make and the source, section or page number where you found relevant information for this			
The successes and failures of the various plans				
The important battles which have taken place				
The new lessons being learnt about warfare				
The casualties				
The morale of the troops				

WORKSHEET 2.1
cont.

You can now write your reports. Your report to the Prime Minister might begin like this.

Military Report – Confidential
Subject: State of war effort
To: Prime Minister Asquith
Date: December 1914
The battle plans
Neither the German nor Allied battle plans have gone as expected. The aim of the German plan was to:

- _____

- _____

- _____

It failed because

- _____

- _____

- _____

(When you write to the PM you can give it to him straight. For the general public you might want to emphasise the role of British troops in the German failure.)

The Allied plan met the following problems:

- _____

- _____

- _____

Now think about how you can organise the other sections in the same way.

What was the fighting like on the Western Front?

AIM

To use a range of sources in context to describe trench warfare

RESOURCES

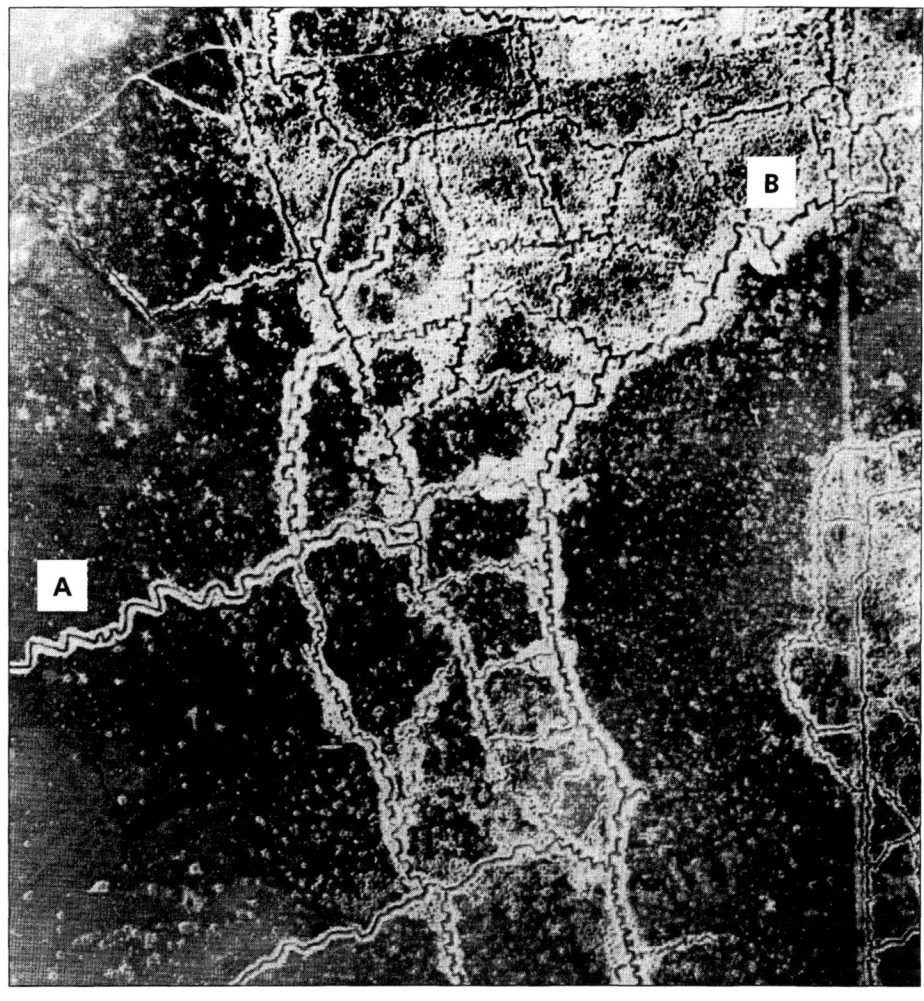

A

1 On this copy of Source 19 from page 23, label the following features:

- frontline trenches
- support trenches
- no-man's land.

2 Explain why you think the trenches are arranged as zig-zag lines, not straight lines.

_____

_____

_____

_____

_____

_____

3 If you had to get from your headquarters behind the lines (marked A) to the frontline position (marked B) how would you get there?

WORKSHEET 2.2 B

cont.

1 Sources 18–20 give you three different kinds of evidence about the trenches: an aerial photograph, a modern reconstruction and two ground-level photographs. Explain for each one how it is useful to a historian.

Use this table to help you:

Source	18	19	20
Brief summary/description			
Reliable source?			
Fits with other sources?			
Fits with own knowledge?			
Conclusion about usefulness			

Source 18 is useful because

• _____

Source 19 is useful because

• _____

Source 20 is useful because

• _____

My own wider knowledge of this topic tells me that the view of the trenches shown by Sources 18–20 is incomplete because

• _____

• _____

However, these sources are still useful because

_____

_____

EXTENSION WORK

You have been asked by the Royal British Legion (the association for former soldiers) to put together a small display page for a Remembrance Day leaflet on what the trenches were like in the Great War. Your display must contain a description of the trenches but due to lack of space (you are limited to one A4 side) you have only 150 words to play with. This does not include headings. You must include at least two visual sources and at least one quote from a serving soldier. (These can be found on pages 26, 30 and 32.)

How did the fighting on the Western Front change?

AIM

To select and use relevant information to explain changes in fighting on the Western Front

RESOURCES

On pages 22–27 you have studied how the equipment and the tactics used on the Western Front were adapted to the realities of trench warfare.

A Work in pairs. You each have to put together advice to be printed in a 'Soldiers' Guide'. You should include advice on tactics and equipment.

One of you should write the guide as it would have appeared in the summer of 1914 as war broke out. The other should write the guide for new recruits coming into the army in 1918.

When you have finished compare your work with that of your partner.

B Write three paragraphs to answer this question:

How did the fighting on the Western Front change?

Paragraph 1 How the war was different from what people expected. (Note down the points you will make in this paragraph.)

- _____

- _____

- _____

Paragraph 2 How techniques and equipment were adapted to trench warfare.

- _____

- _____

- _____

Paragraph 3 Things which did not change and why they did not change.

- _____

- _____

- _____

Turning points on the Western Front

AIM

To organise and deploy information to support a viewpoint

RESOURCES

Historians have disagreed as to what were the turning points on the Western Front. Work in groups. One of you take 1916, one take 1917, the other take 1918. Each of you write a paragraph explaining why your year should be regarded as a turning point in the war. Use the information on pages 28–30 to help you.

Copy this table and use it to put your ideas together for the year you are studying:

Your year 19———	Impact of event on Western Front	Was this event a turning point? (Give reasons)
Key events

1.

2.

3. | | |

Conclusions

I believe that 19… was the crucial year on the Western Front because

- _____
- _____
- _____

I would like to draw attention to these pieces of evidence:

- _____
- _____
- _____

EXTENSION WORK

Copy the grid and in the boxes summarise the key events of each year.

1916	1917	1918
☐	☐	☐
☐	☐	☐
☐	☐	☐
☐	☐	☐

Now decide which of these key events are connected to each other. At first, draw a faint pencil line (in case you want to change your mind) to connect the boxes.

Also, either on the line, or using a number key, write a short explanation of why you believe those events were connected. Your teacher will ask you to justify your lines.

WORKSHEET 2.5 *How was the stalemate broken?*

AIM

To describe and explain how the stalemate was broken

RESOURCES

Look carefully at the chart below. In each column write as many reasons as you can find on pages 28–30. Add any other reasons you can think of.

Why the war became a stalemate	How the stalemate was broken

Draw faint pencil lines (in case you change your mind) to show connections between items in column 1 and column 2.

EXTENSION WORK

Write your own brief account of the war, dividing it into two parts:
Part 1 should explain how and why the war reached stalemate.
Part 2 should explain how and why the stalemate was broken.

You can plan your account by using the diagram below.

Part 1 - Stalemate

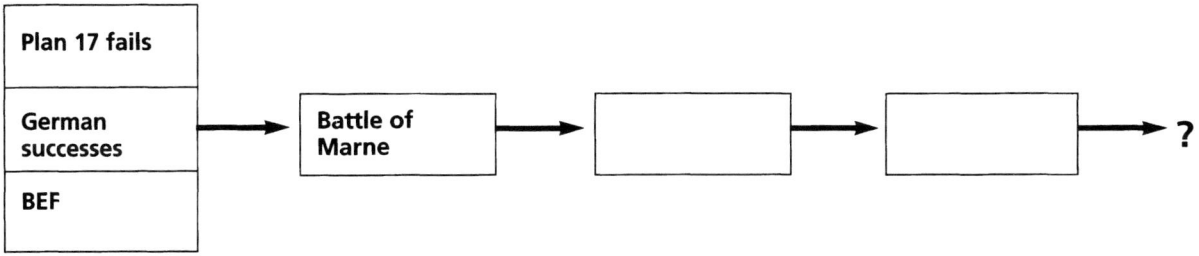

Part 2 - Stalemate broken

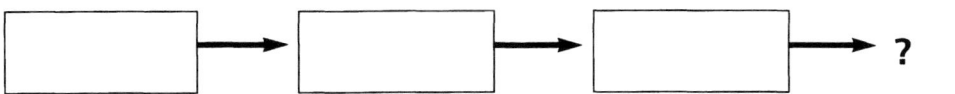

Two of the boxes have been filled in to show part of the process of how the stalemate developed. Fill in the other boxes. You will probably need to add more boxes of your own.

How was the war portrayed?

AIM

To evaluate different interpretations of the war

RESOURCES

1 Look back over pages 31–34 and find examples of each of the following kinds of sources about the war.

Kind of source	Example	How does it portray the war?
Poem		
An advertisement		
Painting		
Magazine illustration		
Newspaper article		
Cartoon		
Diary		
Novel		

2 Choose the two sources which you think are the most realistic. Explain your choice.

3 Choose two which are unrealistic. Explain your choice.

4 From what you know about the war explain why representations of it vary so greatly.

EXTENSION WORK

'On the whole, people in Britain received an accurate picture of what the war was like.' Explain whether you agree with this statement, referring to the sources you chose for questions 1–4 above to support what you say.

Different fronts in the First World War

AIM

To examine the similarities and differences between the fighting on the Western and other fronts

RESOURCES

As you look at Part 2 of Chapter 2 make sure that this table is within easy reach. By the time you reach the end of Part 2 you should have made a list of the similarities and differences between the Western Front and the other areas where fighting took place.

Keep looking back over your work in order to fill in parts of the chart. As well as giving yourself a useful picture of the fighting, you will find that this process of looking back will help with your revision.

	Front		
	Gallipoli	Balkans and Middle East	Russian (Eastern) Front
Similarities to the Western Front			
Differences from the Western Front			

EXTENSION WORK

Did the fighting on the other fronts in the First World War follow the same pattern as that on the Western Front? Answer this question in about 150–200 words. Refer to movement of troops, use of new technology, weapons and tactics, local factors (local peoples, geographical features, weather).

Here is a possible framework for your answer:

There were similarities and differences between the various fronts. The Western Front began as a war of movement and then became bogged down in trench warfare.

GALLIPOLI
The Gallipoli campaign was similar to the Western Front in that

• _____

But there were important differences:

• _____

BALKANS AND MIDDLE EAST
This campaign was similar in that

• _____

But the differences were:

• _____

RUSSIAN (EASTERN) FRONT
This campaign was similar to the Western Front in that

• _____

But it was different because

• _____

GCSE Modern World History

The Gallipoli campaign

To describe the key features of the Gallipoli campaign and explain why it was a failure

Work in pairs.

You are historical researchers. In the Focus Task on page 37 you have been given two questions to investigate:

- Why was the Gallipoli campaign a failure?
- Why were the casualties so high?

Take one question each.

Before you present the answers to these questions you must do some planning.

Your aim is effective use of sources, to examine causes.

1 What source material will each of you use for your particular question?

2 How much time do you have for your research? Don't spend all your time on just one source.

3 How are you expected to present your conclusions?

For each question you need to use examples to explain:

- Things which went wrong
- Why they went wrong
- Whether the problems could have been predicted and avoided.

You may find the following grid helpful in planning your answer:

Source/text section	What it says about ...	Things which went wrong	Why they went wrong	Whether this problem could have been avoided

2.9

How important was Russia's role in the war?

AIM

To select and deploy information relevant to the issue of Russia's contribution to the Allied war effort

RESOURCES

Which of these statements from the Focus Task on page 40 do you most agree with?

Statement 1 Russia did not help the Allies win the war. It withdrew from the war before the Allies won.

Statement 2 Russia tied up millions of German and Austrian troops on the Eastern Front. Without that the Allies would not have won the war.

Statement 1
List any events, examples or pieces of evidence you can find which support this statement.

_____

_____

_____

_____

_____

Statement 2
List any events, examples or pieces of evidence you can find which support this statement.

_____

_____

_____

_____

_____

Conclusion
Decide which statement is best supported by the evidence.

_____

_____

_____

_____

_____

_____

_____

_____

The Great War on all fronts

AIM

To record the main events of the different fronts in the war

RESOURCES

All of the events you have read about on pages 35–41 were happening at the same time as the events you have studied on the Western Front.

On the table below, insert into the correct places all the dated events mentioned on pages 35–41. This will help you in preparing your timeline on page 41.

	1914	1915	1916	1917	1918
The Western Front	Schlieffen Plan; Ypres		Verdun; Somme	Cambrai (tanks)	Ludendorff Offensive; Allied counter attack
Other fronts Gallipoli The Balkans The Middle East The Russian Front The war at sea					

EXTENSION WORK

In small groups, give each of the fronts a rating on a scale of 1–10 in terms of how important that front was in deciding the outcome of the war (10 is most important). Now compare your views with those of other groups.

Finally, explain in your own words why it is not really possible to have the 'right answer' in this type of exercise.

How was Britain organised to fight the Great War?

AIM

To use a source in context to explain the impact of war on British families

RESOURCES

Between 1914 and 1918 the war reached into every corner of people's lives. Family members were killed. Food was rationed. Freedom was restricted. Civilians faced danger. The source below shows one cartoonist's view of the impact of the war on a British family.

1A _____

1B _____

1C _____

1D _____

1 Write a detailed description of what each frame shows in the chart below. Point out anything which has changed since the last frame.

Cartoon	Description	Changes	Why?
1A			
1B			
1C			
1D			

2 From what you have found out about life on the Home Front explain in the fourth column why these changes have taken place.

3 Write a phrase to sum up the family's attitude to the war in each year and write it by the relevant cartoon on the previous page. You could choose one of the following phrases or write one of your own: Grim determination; Hard times; Wartime spirit; Let's get organised.

EXTENSION WORK

1 Do you think this cartoon is an accurate representation of the attitudes of British people through war time? Explain your answer fully by referring to:

- the aspects of life in war time which the cartoon depicts
- how far these aspects are shown accurately (remember, even humorous cartoons can still be accurate, although they often exaggerate the true picture)
- aspects of wartime life which the cartoon does not cover.

2 Write a description, or draw a picture of what the cartoonist might have drawn at the end of 1918.

What was the impact of the war on women?

AIM

To describe and explain the extent of change in British women's lives as a result of the war

RESOURCES

1 Look back over pages 55–57. Use the grid below to make a list of the key areas in which the war changed the lives of women and the areas where little changed (where there was 'continuity').

Areas	Change	Continuity
Work		
Votes		
Place in society		

2 Write a paragraph to explain which of these three statements you most agree with.

a) The war made very little change to the lives of women.

b) The war speeded up changes that were taking place already.

c) The war changed the role of women enormously.

The peace treaties after the First World War

Key features of the chapter

	Issue covered	Assessment elements	Format(s) for pupil work
Activity: Opinions in 1919	British public opinion on the treaties	Key features of an historical situation	Analysis and criticism of a key source
Focus Task (p. 62): Paris Peace Conference	What were the aims of the leaders at the Conference?	Selecting and deploying information, key features of an historical situation	Structured research and recording
Activity (p. 63): The Fourteen Points	Views of the other leaders on Wilson's ideas	Use of sources, selecting and deploying information	Comparison of views, reconstructed letter
Focus Task (p. 65): Allied leaders at Versailles	Why did the Allied leaders not get the Treaty they wanted?	Selecting and deploying, information, describing and analysing issues	Structured research and extended writing
Focus Task (p. 67): Terms of the Treaty	Could the Treaty of Versailles be justified at the time?	Use of sources, selecting and deploying information	Views of contemporaries on the terms of the treaty
Focus Task (p. 67): Versailles Treaty and Germany	What was the impact of the Treaty of Versailles on Germany?	Selecting and deploying information, describing and analysing events	Letter from Berlin
Focus Task (p. 71): Other treaties after the war	How fair were the peace treaties?	Describing and analysing events	Rating treaties and extended writing
Focus Task (p. 73): Czechoslovakia	What were the strengths and weaknesses of the new Czechoslovakia?	Use of sources	Substantiated list of strengths and weaknesses

The Paris Peace Conference – the Issue Starter

Source 1 shows the eagerness with which Allied officers and officials strained to see the signing of the Treaty. This is an ideal opportunity to introduce a whole-class question and answer session.

1 Does Source 1 show the sort of behaviour you normally expect from officers and officials?

2 Why are they so eager to see the ceremony?

– Is it that they simply find it hard to believe that the war is over?

– Do they have doubts that the Germans will sign the Treaty?

– Do they simply want to see the Germans get what is coming to them?

Source 2 shows the popularity of the leaders after the announcement of the Treaty. Again it offers the possibility for a range of questions.

1 Does anyone recognise any of the figures (especially if they have studied the First World War)?

2 How is the crowd reacting to them?

3 If you were a journalist of the time, what caption would you write for this photograph?

The future criticisms of the Treaty of Versailles could be briefly referred to and contrasted with the image in Source 2.

The mood in 1919

This section has two purposes. The first is to draw a link with the preceding two chapters which deal respectively with the blame for starting the war and the subsequent horrors of the war once it did begin. The questions on page 59 are suitable for whole-class discussion or as written exercises. The second purpose is to introduce pupils to a range of issues which dominate world history for the next twenty years.

Some pupils may need guidance with the **Activity (page 60)** based around **Source 5**. They will find it helpful to look at the context of the source and to be reminded of the intense anti-German feeling during the election campaign of 1918. They may find the following hints useful for writing their paragraph on why Germany ought to be treated harshly:

1 Responsibility for the war
2 The human cost
3 The cost in terms of money
4 The damage done to Belgium and France
5 The Treaty of Brest–Litovsk.

The second part of the Activity might work best as an oral follow-up after one or two pupils have summarised their paragraphs. Pupils might work in small groups to put together questions and criticisms and the teacher could put him/herself in the 'hot seat' as Sir Eric Geddes.

The aims of the leaders

This section builds up to the first of the Focus Tasks. **Worksheet 3.1** provides a template for recording answers, although it may be more useful if pupils draw their own to fit the dimensions of their file or exercise book. (Don't forget the extra column.) Pupils will probably find it helpful to draw up the diagram or look at the template before they read the chapter. This way they will bear the task in mind as they read.

The three cartoons on **page 62** form the basis of an extension activity for which a template is also provided (**Worksheet 3.2**). This exercise offers the opportunity for pupils to look at cartoons in their historical context and to try to link these sources with the feelings and opinions which must have been prevalent at the time. The aim is also to introduce pupils to a structured way of looking at this difficult type of source.

The **Activity** on **page 63** is designed to get pupils to discuss and work with the Fourteen Points, and in doing so become familiar with them. Again, a template is provided for the activity (**Worksheet 3.3**), along with some prompts to help pupils to write their letters to President Wilson.

The Treaty of Versailles

This is a large and vitally important section of the chapter, and indeed of the book as a whole. The aim of the major **Focus Task** on **page 65** is for pupils to become familiar with the key terms, issues and points of the Treaty by processing and using the information in this section. Pupils could first read through pages 63–64 on their own, in preparation for the Focus Task. Teachers might want to set up an informal simulation, in which the pupils put themselves in the position of people from the time listening to the terms being read out on a radio broadcast. Both teacher and pupils could take on the role of reporters/broadcasters.

Section A of the Focus Task challenges pupils to identify the compromises which must have taken place at the Conference. Although each pupil is asked to look at one leader they will receive feedback on the other leaders from fellow pupils. Writing up these sections would make a very suitable piece of homework.

Section C demands a piece of extended writing. It is entirely flexible in that pupils could be asked to repeat the process for all of the statements, which would in the end amount to a balanced essay. For pupils who have difficulty in writing at length, the structure given on **Worksheet 3.4** may prove helpful.

German reactions to the Treaty

This section opens up opportunities for work with sources in which pupils can deepen their understanding of the issue and lay the ground for understanding the rise of the Nazis in Germany in later years. Sources 12, 13, 14 and 15 provide pupils with a snapshot of Germany in 1919. The value of this evidence can be addressed in a question such as 'Do Sources 12–15 provide reliable evidence for historians about the reaction of the majority of Germans to the Treaty of Versailles?'.

Guidance points:

1 Do all of the sources seem to suggest the same reaction to the Treaty?

2 Would you agree that they represent the views of the majority of Germans or is it not possible to say?

3 Does this picture fit with your own knowledge of the reaction to the Treaty in Germany?

4 What evidence could you bring to support your answer to this question?

The first **Focus Task** on **page 67** addresses the question of whether the Treaty could be justified at the time, and is encouraging pupils to develop a sense of historical perspective. Some pupils may find it helpful to be given a little extra direction in locating sources and the sections of the text relevant to their allotted task. Others may find it more fruitful to use the index or simply skim the text.

- Belgian civilian: see Chapter 2 (pages 17–23; Source 3, page 59)
- British person: see Chapter 2 (pages 46–54, 59 and 61; Sources 4, 5 and 7)
- French politician: see page 60 (Clemenceau profile); Sources 8, 9 and 10 on page 62.

For the **Focus Task** at the bottom of page 67 pupils should be encouraged to think a little about the type of German they might be when they write their letter. So many shades of opinion were represented in Germany immediately after the war that it might be worth spending some time building up the viewpoint of the writer, using some of the prompts below:

1 The age of the writer (a young person might see things differently from an older German who could possibly have lost sons and grandsons in the war)

2 Whether the writer supported the government or one of the groups which tried to overthrow it

3 Whether he or she belonged to the middle classes

4 Why is the French and Belgian occupation of the Ruhr unjustified?

5 If you were writing to a relative in the USA you might well be a German Jew – how are you being treated?

6 What sort of problems would inflation cause for simple tasks like going shopping?

The final **Activity** in this section, on **page 69**, might work best as a discussion activity. Again, the aim is to hypothesise in a constructive way, exploring the options which were open to the leaders at the time.

The other peace settlements

These lesser settlements are not treated in as much depth as the Treaty of Versailles. The emphasis in this section is on introducing pupils to the terms of the treaties in outline, and on familiarising them with the geography of eastern Europe in particular. As well as enhancing their understanding of this issue, it provides invaluable grounding for the problems of the League of Nations and Hitler's aggressive policies in the 1930s.

The Focus Task on page 71 gives the chance to reinforce understanding of the Treaty of Versailles as well as look at the other agreements. An effective strategy would be for small groups or pairs to discuss the grading of the treaties and then report back in a teacher-led whole session. A recording template has been provided on **Worksheet 3.5**. The two versions allow for pupils to revise their views in the light of feedback from the teacher and the rest of the group.

The final **Focus Task** in this section (**pages 73–74**) lends itself to individual investigation followed up by an extended piece of writing in the form of a report. This could be presented as if by an historian or perhaps as a report from a commentator at the time. Some useful guidance is provided on **Worksheet 3.6**.

The aims of the leaders at the Paris Peace Conference

AIM

To examine and summarise the aims of the leaders at the Paris Peace Conference

RESOURCES

Leader	Country	Attitude to Germany	Main aims	
Clemenceau				
Lloyd George				
Wilson				

WORSHEET

3.2

Viewpoints on the Paris Peace Conference

AIM

To evaluate key sources in their historical context

RESOURCES

Cartoons are still used in newspapers today, but they are much less important now than they were in 1920. Cartoons originated in the 1700s. The aim of the first cartoons was to make political points and make fun of politicians at a time when the great majority of the population was not able to read. In the 1920s there was no television and cartoons were still an important way of making points in a visual way which was easy for people to understand.

Because we are looking at cartoons many years after they were made, it can sometimes be difficult to spot all of the points which the cartoonist was trying to make when the cartoon was drawn. Use the following pointers to help you when you look at a cartoon:

Background
- The date it was drawn – what else was going on at the same time?
- The country and the type of publication in which the cartoon was published (e.g. a British newspaper which supported a harsh treaty).

Words
- Look at the caption (if the cartoon has one) – it is usually very important.
- Many cartoons use labels on the characters or include objects. Look very carefully for these as they give very strong clues as to what the cartoon is about.

The cartoon itself
- Start by looking at the background if there is one – what impression is it trying to give?
- Look at any figures and think about how the cartoonist has drawn them in terms of size, bulk and their position in relation to each other.
- Facial expressions are usually very important – they tell you whether the cartoonist thinks that a character is brave, cowardly, sincere, treacherous etc.

We have analysed Source 10 on the next sheet (from page 62 of the Pupil Book) for you to show you how this can be done.

EXTENSION WORK

1 Use the formula above to analyse Sources 8 and 9 on page 62. Write a short commentary on each one.
2 Do you feel that Sources 8–10 accurately reflect the mood in 1919? Explain your answer by referring to the events of 1919 and the views of people and politicians of the time.
3 The year is 1919. Decide whether you support a harsh or moderate treaty and then either:
   a) Draw your own cartoon supporting your view
   b) Design a cartoon and write accurate instructions to an artist.
   Your cartoon should include:
   • a background
   • a caption – preferably using sarcasm or humour
   • figures who can be clearly recognised
   • labels on the cartoon itself to help people understand the point you are trying to make.

An example of how a cartoon can be analysed

Facial expression shows determination

French and British police:
- Civilian (war is over)
- Large and capable – will accept no nonsense from Germany

Background shows destruction of war

Facial expression (along with the words in the caption) suggests he is sly and cunning

Although beaten, Germany is shown as solid and potentially dangerous – not as weak

The aim of the terms (in the cartoonist's view) is clear from the rope binding Germany, which reads 'Armistice terms'

Caption: makes it plain what the cartoonist thinks

PUNCH, OR THE LONDON CHARIVARI.—FEBRUARY 19, 1919.

GIVING HIM ROPE?

GERMAN CRIMINAL (*to Allied Police*). "HERE, I SAY, STOP! YOU'RE HURTING ME! [*Aside*]
IF I ONLY WHINE ENOUGH I MAY BE ABLE TO WRIGGLE OUT OF THIS YET."

The cartoon is by a famous cartoonist, Bernard Partridge. Look back at Chapter 2 for other cartoons of his.

WORSHEET *The Fourteen Points*

3.3

AIM

To describe and explain the Fourteen Points and the attitudes of other leaders to them

RESOURCES

A Work in groups. Fill in this table to show what views
a) Clemenceau; and
b) Lloyd George
would have expressed on points 2, 4, 5, 8, 10 and 14 of the Fourteen Points on page 61.

Points	Clemenceau	Lloyd George
2 Free seas		
4 Disarmament		
5 Colonies		
8 Alsace–Lorraine		
10 Eastern Europe		
14 League of Nations		

B On your own, write a letter from one of the two leaders to Wilson summarising your views on the Fourteen Points.

Dear President Wilson

I have now had the chance to look carefully at your Fourteen Points and I would like to express my views on a number of the points in particular.

Point 2
I believe that this point is

* _____

* _____

* _____

Point 5
I believe that this point is

* _____

* _____

* _____

etc etc
Yours sincerely
Lloyd George/Clemenceau

Why did the Big Three not get what they wanted?

AIM

To select and deploy relevant information to support an historical interpretation

RESOURCES

Choose one of the following phrases to finish off this sentence:
The Big Three did not all get the Treaty they wanted because …
Option 1 Clemenceau bullied Wilson and Lloyd George into agreeing a harsh treaty.
Option 2 The leaders were too different – they could not all have got what they wanted and someone was bound to be disappointed.
Option 3 Public opinion in their home countries affected the leaders' decisions.

I believe that the reason why the Big Three did not all get the Treaty they wanted was …

_____

I chose this option because

* _____

* _____

* _____

The evidence to support my choice is that

* _____

* _____

* _____

There is also evidence to support options … and …

* _____

* _____

* _____

However, on balance I believe that option … is the best answer because …

_____

_____

_____

_____

_____

_____

_____

_____

_____

_____

WORKSHEET

3.5

Were the peace treaties fair?

In this chapter you have investigated a number of different treaties. Choose two treaties and score them on a scale of 1 to 5 for fairness. 1 is very fair, 5 is very unfair.

For each treaty write a paragraph to explain why you gave it the score you did.

You might find it helpful to use this table to look back briefly at all of the treaties before you choose the two treaties you are going to write about.

AIM

To examine the terms of the treaties and reach a supported judgement on them

RESOURCES

Treaty	Date	Rating	Comments
Versailles		1 2 3 4 5	
St Germain		1 2 3 4 5	
Trianon		1 2 3 4 5	
Neuilly		1 2 3 4 5	
Sèvres		1 2 3 4 5	

WORKSHEET

3.6

What were the strengths and weaknesses of the new Czechoslovakia?

AIM

To describe and explain the strengths and weaknesses of Czechoslovakia in 1920

RESOURCES

Look at the sources in the Focus Task on pages 73–74, and fill out this table to help you analyse the strengths and weaknesses of the new country of Czechoslovakia.

Source	What does it tell you about Czechoslovakia's • borders • industry • population?	Suggests weakness or strength?	Comments (e.g. on reliability of source)
26			
27			
28			
29			
30			
31			

SECTION 2: THE USSR, GERMANY AND THE USA BETWEEN THE WARS

4 Russia and the USSR 1905–1941

Key features of the chapter

	Issue covered	Assessment elements	Format(s) for pupil work
Activity (p. 80): Russia 1903	Status of Russia in 1903	Selecting and deploying information	Report from Tsar's ministers
Focus Task (p. 82): The 1905 revolution	How did the Tsar survive the 1905 revolution?	Key features of historical situation, selecting and deploying information	Annotated diagram
Focus Task (p. 83): Russia's government	How well was Russia governed?	Describing and analysing events	List of substantiated judgements on Russia's government
Focus Task (p. 85): The impact of the First World War	How did the First World War weaken the Tsar's government?	Use of sources	Structured writing
Focus Task (p. 85): Revolution	Why did the Tsarist regime collapse in 1917?	Describe and explain events and changes	Annotated diagram followed by extended writing
Focus Task (p. 87): The Provisional Government	How effective was the Provisional Government?	Describe and explain events and changes	Structured writing
Focus Task (p. 89): The Bolshevik Revolution	Why were the Bolsheviks successful?	Use of sources, selecting and deploying information	Extended writing
Focus Task (p. 94): The Civil War	Why did the Bolsheviks win the Civil War?	Describe and explain key events and issues	Poster
Focus Task (p. 97): Bolshevik rule	How did the Bolsheviks consolidate their rule?	Describe and explain key events and issues	Annotated timeline and extended writing
Focus Task (p. 99): Stalin's rise	Why did Stalin win?	Use of sources, selecting and deploying information	Radio feature
Focus Task (p. 100): Five-Year Plans	Why did Stalin introduce the Five-Year Plans?	Key features of an historical situation	Two lists – public and private agenda for plans
Activity (p. 104): Impact of Five-Year Plans	Glory to Stalin and misery to the people?	Use of sources, selecting and deploying information	Discussion, letter
Focus Task (p. 105): Stalin's policies	Stalin's economic policies: success or failure?	Describing, analysing and explaining events	Annotated diagram and extended writing
Focus Task (p. 108): Stalin's USSR	How did Stalin control the USSR?	Selecting and deploying information, describing, analysing and explaining events	Recording template, extended writing
Focus Task (p. 108): Stalin	Stalin: success or failure?	Use of sources, selecting and deploying information, describing, analysing and explaining events	Class debate

Part 1 HOW DID THE BOLSHEVIKS TAKE CONTROL?

The coronation of the new Tsar – the Issue Starter

To establish the extent of devotion to the Tsar, pupils could take the opening paragraph of this section and the photograph **(Source 1, page 76)** and consider the following questions:

1 How popular did the Russian monarchy appear to be?
2 Do the British royal family generate these sorts of scenes today?
3 Who would draw the sort of crowds seen in the photograph?

They could then see how the relationship between the Tsar and his people took a turn for the worse in the incidents of Bloody Sunday. Pupils could look at the **three visual sources (Sources 11–13)** and compare these scenes with that in Source 1.

The new Tsar

In order to appreciate the forthcoming transformation and to make contrasts pupils need to get a feel for how uniquely backward Russia was amongst all of the great powers of the day. This section aims to look at the real and apparent strength of the Tsarist system. By looking in some depth at the nature of Russia at the turn of the century pupils can begin to understand what Russia and Russians were like. By examining the Tsarist system and its opponents they can begin to make their own 'interim' judgements on the efficacy of the system and whether they feel at this stage that it was doomed. The section concludes with an Activity (page 80) which is designed to get pupils to bring all of their findings together and show their understanding of the material they have studied.

Question 1 on page 77 is well suited to a discussion between teacher and whole class. Teachers may feel it worthwhile to use **Worksheet 4.1** to chart the fortunes of the Tsar from 1900 to 1917. Pupils could use the sheet as a reference point across all of the first three sections, using the Tsar as a fixed point in the tide of events. The finished product should give them a useful summary sheet of the last years of Tsarist rule. **Worksheet 4.1** also provides support for **question 2** on **page 77**. Whatever the final method of dealing with the questions the key issue for pupils to grasp is the fundamental unsuitability of the Tsar for his position, especially at the time when Russia was so clearly at a crossroads.

Questions 1 and 2 on page 79 address the question of the state of Russia itself rather than the Tsarist system. The questions could be tackled either as written or discussion tasks. However, they will probably be of greatest value as preparation exercises for the Activity on page 80. If they are used for this purpose it would be advisable for pupils to be warned in advance so that they can organise their thinking accordingly. **Question 1** on **page 80** should also be seen as a preparation for the activity – the pupils should know who the groups are, what they stand for and what they are against.

The Activity on page 80 should enable pupils to bring all of their work and reading from this section together and to get a clear picture of what Russia was like around the turn of the century. The essence of the Activity is that pupils are working with information, processing and using it rather than simply moving it from one location to another. **Worksheet 4.2** provides a framework which some pupils might find helpful.

The 1905 revolution

In the questions and tasks in this section the emphasis is very much on pupils looking at sources analytically and using them to test ideas about the 1905 revolution and to come up with ideas of their own. **Questions 3–7** on **page 81** are best suited to written responses and ask pupils to show their understanding of the sources and the context in which they are set.

In **question 3** the process of making a list is important as it involves pupils either searching for key words in the document or finding suitable words of their own to summarise grievances. Either process involves close study of the text of the source. **Questions 4 and 5** ask pupils to show their understanding of the context by drawing out the style and tone of the petition. **Questions 6 and 7** remind pupils of one of the themes of this chapter: the transformation of attitudes in Russia. Question 6 indicates clearly the change of heart undergone by Father Gapon in the light of the Bloody Sunday incident. Question 7 reinforces this but also asks pupils to look at different perspectives on the events of Bloody Sunday. In order to explain the differences between the depictions pupils might find the following hints helpful:

• The size of the crowd and the way it is shown (peaceful, rowdy)
• The distance between the troops and the crowd
• The angle from which the events are shown
• The date of each source and the type of source in each case.

As an extension or follow-up exercise pupils could look back at their answers as well as the text and answer the following question in a piece of extended writing:

'Bloody Sunday was the result of

• the Tsar's troops putting down a violent uprising
• ruthless and insensitive overreaction by the Tsar
• frightened soldiers overreacting to the size of the crowd.'

Which of these three explanations seems to fit best with the evidence? Explain your answer by referring to the evidence for and against each one in turn and then writing a conclusion.

The Focus Task on page 82 is supported by **Worksheet 4.3**. The aim of this task is to identify the factors which enabled the Tsar to stay in power and crush the revolution. By putting these factors into a diagram, pupils are extracting key points from the body of text and equipping themselves with a visual reminder which should be a helpful revision aid.

It would be useful to remind pupils that, while reading the section following the Focus Task, they should note down the measures taken by the Tsar's ministers to stay in control (rather than simply regaining control). Indeed, it might well be a useful exercise for pairs or small groups to read through this section together as it contains a great deal of important information. Teachers may want to be sure that relevant details have been gleaned by holding a whole-class feedback session in which pupils compare the final contents of their diagrams.

The Focus Task on page 83 is supported by **Worksheet 4.4**. It provides a framework for analysing the performance of the Tsarist government. However, it should be used to come back to at different stages, for pupils to analyse Bolshevik and Stalinist rule. This should provide pupils with a thorough overview of Russia in this period, and be a careful revision too!

War and revolution

The main focus in this section is on the collapse of the Tsarist system. The two Focus Tasks in the section address the issue of the impact of the First World War and the effects of the war on top of the problems already facing Russia in 1914. Pupils should aim to use the wide range of sources provided to reach their own conclusions. However, there should also be a strong emphasis on pupils using the accompanying text to validate or challenge the impressions given by the sources.

The text itself builds up the picture of a Russia being relentlessly worn down by the demands of war, but it also stresses the continuing problem of incompetent government at home. **Questions 1 and 2** on **page 84** could be used to elicit this in discussion. Pupils could then go on to use **Worksheet 4.5** for the smaller **Focus Task** on **page 85**. Using the framework suggested, pupils can search the sources for relevant evidence, check the validity of that evidence and then turn their findings into a written answer to the question.

The larger **Focus Task** on **page 85** is rather more wide-ranging and requires pupils to look at the immediate causes of the revolution. The key objectives in part A are that:

- the factors which pupils identify are correct
- the lines they draw to show connections can be justified with examples or with reference to sources.

For part B pupils will need to refer back to their work on the **Focus Task** on **page 82** to draw conclusions about why the 1917 revolution succeeded where the 1905 revolution had failed. In this part the key objective is to identify and compare the causal factors in 1905 and 1917 and to justify the choice of the key reason for success in 1917. The extension activity is aimed at developing pupils' ability to structure and maintain a line of argument, but also to use different types of evidence to support that argument. **Worksheets 4.6a and 4.6b** contain a range of devices to support students in their work.

The Provisional Government

Question 1 on page 86 goes straight to the heart of the matter of the actions of the Provisional Government in 1917. The question could be usefully tackled as written work but it does offer the opportunity for pupils to speculate, even before they read the relevant section of the book, on such questions as:

- For whose benefit is the Provisional Government ruling?
- How long do you think it will last with policies like these? (A swift look at Source 27 will sharpen pupils' thinking on this.)

The overall emphasis of this section is on a government struggling against enormous odds and determined to pursue policies it believed to be for the good of the country but which were unpopular with the majority of the people. The **Focus Task** on **page 87** directs pupils to these issues and **Worksheet 4.7** provides guidance and structure for this. Again, the thrust of the task is to synthesise the narrative drive of the text with a range of related sources. The extension activities demand that pupils extend their view back to the previous section. This will encourage them to think further about the characteristics of good government. It will also encourage them to look at the extent to which the Provisional Government was representative of the people. This should provide a helpful perspective when pupils study Bolshevik rule later in the chapter.

The Bolshevik Revolution

There are two themes running through this section. The first, which is worth stressing with pupils, is that the Bolsheviks claimed that the legitimacy for their rule came from the 'fact' that they had led a popular revolution in 1917. This section asks pupils to recognise that this was really not the case.

Secondly, there is the question of how, when they were a minority group, the Bolsheviks were able to seize power. This issue is addressed by concentrating on the role and qualities of Lenin in the **Activity** on **page 89**. This activity asks pupils to delve deeply into a small number of relevant sources and pull out references to Lenin's qualities. **Worksheet 4.8** provides a framework which they can use to extend the profile of Lenin and keep in their exercise books.

Worksheet 4.9 asks pupils to write at some length and to use a range of sources to answer a simple but extremely important question. For weaker pupils in particular, the task is broken down into three stages:

1 The diagram helps pupils to pull together the other 'mighty factors' into one place and think about how they will manage them. Some pupils may find it helpful to have starter hints about these mighty forces:

- The changes which had been taking place in Russia since 1900 (rapid growth of the Russian urban working classes; poor living and working conditions; disillusionment with the Tsar)
- Suspicion of the middle-class Kerensky and his Provisional Government (land reform; the war)
- The dreadful effects of the war (casualties; food prices; mismanagement; mutiny in the army)
- The activities of the Bolsheviks.

2 Having 'brainstormed' the possible elements to be inserted into their answer pupils can then use the planning grid to decide how their answers will be ordered, how they will contribute to the answer to the question and the supporting evidence or examples they will use. Teachers may wish to alter the parameters for their pupils (e.g. primary sources only) to suit their needs.

3 The writing frame should then help pupils to write a coherent answer to the question.

Part 2 LENIN'S RUSSIA

Lenin in power

This section centres on the changes brought about by Lenin and the Bolsheviks as they transformed the country from Russia into the USSR. The key themes of Russia in transition and Bolshevik rule run through all of the subsections and the Focus Tasks.

Question 1 on page 90 attempts to go straight to the heart of the matter. A written or oral response would be appropriate here, but the question sets up the possibility for a short discussion with the pupils before they go on to look at Bolshevik rule:

1 On the basis of the Factfile only, what impression do you get of the Bolsheviks (e.g. their attitudes to ordinary working people, protecting the new state and redistributing wealth)?

2 Does this view tally with what you have already read about Lenin and the Bolsheviks?

Worksheet 4.10 is not attached to a Focus Task but might be a useful exercise to help students see how the unfolding events of the revolution affected Russian people. If the empathetic aim is not feasible, students can still write from the perspective of the modern historian about how events would affect Vladimir.

The following sections could then be used for **Worksheet 4.9**. Pupils could read about the establishment of the Bolshevik dictatorship and the Treaty of Brest–Litovsk and record their feelings as they read. They may even want to address the hypothetical question of which side they would support on the outbreak of Civil War. **Questions 1 and 2** on **page 92** complement this by asking pupils to work with the sources on the Civil War. In fact, these questions could link in with **Worksheet 4.10** by asking pupils to explain whether (and why) their opinion has changed or not changed at the end of the Civil War.

For questions 1 and 2 themselves, some pupils might find it helpful to organise their answers into headings. For question 1 they could group their findings under food; law and order; business and the economy; work; killings. For question 2 they might find it helpful to break the source into its component parts: background scene; size and position of figures; actions shown in the picture. From these points they should be able to reach a conclusion which they can support.

Why did the Bolsheviks win?

This section deals with a question which demands answers beyond the simple military explanations. **Question 3** on **page 93** and **questions 1 and 2** on **page 94** address this issue. Questions 3 and 1 would work well as discussion stimuli. Question 2 could also be used in this way, but would be equally suitable for a written answer or even a piece of homework or mini examination question.

These questions should provide pupils with a few insights and ideas for the **Focus Task** relating to this section (**page 94**). There are several objectives in this task:

• Researching and identifying reasons for Bolshevik success
• Assessing the aims, motives, style and methods of Bolshevik propaganda
• Giving pupils the opportunity to show understanding in a medium other than writing.

It is important to stress to pupils that a poster is not a soft option. In the first instance, pupils who are really uncomfortable with drawing could be given the option of writing detailed guidance for the artist who will draw the poster. To create a good poster, pupils must set out the aims of their poster and how they see these aims being achieved. This implies really sophisticated levels of understanding and interpretation of primary source material. **Worksheet 4.11** provides guidance for this task.

The New Economic Policy

As pupils look at War Communism and the NEP teachers may want to remind them about **Worksheet 4.14**. War Communism needs careful explanation since although pupils can readily grasp the necessity for wartime requisitioning, the role of War Communism in creating a Communist society is often less clear. **Questions 3–5** on **page 95** are source-based questions which address the impact of War Communism on ordinary Russians. They could be usefully tackled as written exercises as they foreshadow the reasons for the introduction of the NEP.

There are two points to note about the diagrams on **page 96**. It is important to stress to pupils that the figures in **Source 17** are examples only, to show how War Communism and the NEP worked in principle. Secondly, you will probably need to explain that an 'index' (**Source 20**) is a scale by means of which variable items such as the cost of living can be measured against each other or a base figure.

Question 1 on page 97 again asks pupils to try to draw conclusions from source material. **Sources 18–21** provide a useful bank of source material for further work on the NEP. A suggested set of extension questions is provided below.

1 Read Source 18. According to Lenin, why is the NEP necessary?
2 In what ways do Lenin's views on the NEP differ from those of Bukharin in Source 19?
3 Which of Sources 20 and 21 would you regard as more useful to an historian studying the NEP? Explain your answer.
4 'The NEP was an economic failure.' Do Sources 19–21 and your own knowledge of the period support this view? Explain your answer.

The death of Lenin and the creation of the USSR

This short final section aims to bring together the revolutionary and Bolshevik periods along with a brief assessment of Lenin. **Worksheet 4.12** combines the **Focus Task** on **page 97** with the assessment of Lenin (in greater depth) and an opportunity to review the government of Russia across the period.

Part 3 STALIN – SUCCESS OR FAILURE?

Stalin or Trotsky?

The figure of Stalin towers over this section of the chapter. The text attempts to interleave the complexities of the period with the character of Stalin himself. His personality therefore features heavily in this opening section, which should be referred back to when pupils try to analyse Stalin's motives in later tasks.

This should be made easier if pupils tackle **questions 1 and 3** on **pages 98 and 99** in a written form, perhaps enhanced by visual images. It is important to remember that these are not second-rate activities. To produce a *good* flier pupils must have a subtle grasp of the issues involved in becoming leader of the Bolsheviks after Lenin. **Question 2** is meant to balance the one-sided picture generated by the flier.

A similar principle is applied in the combination of **question 3** and the **Activity** on **page 99**. The flier exercise for Stalin will result in pupils extracting Stalin's better qualities as well as Trotsky's foibles. **Worksheet 4.13** provides support for the activity itself and also offers the opportunity to turn the activity into a piece of extended writing.

Worksheet 4.14 provides a story board to help pupils plan and execute their radio broadcast. The emphasis of the activity is very much on bringing disparate pieces of evidence together to create a coherent and structured narrative.

Modernising the USSR

This section returns to the theme of transformation. Teachers will probably find it worthwhile to read through **Source 4** on **page 100** with pupils as it contains so many points which are central to an understanding of Stalin's attempts to modernise the USSR. The key point to stress is clearly the relationship between security and industrial development.

The Focus Task on page 100 is supported by **Worksheet 4.15** which provides an alternative method of tackling the information and sources so that pupils reach their own conclusions about the true purpose of the Five-Year Plans, and how this differs from the stated or official purpose.

Questions 1–4 on page 102 target the issue of how far the Five-Year Plans succeeded. They also ask pupils to focus on statistics as source material. **Worksheet 4.16** contains a framework for answering the questions. The worksheet also contains an extended writing activity to get pupils thinking about the different types of sources available to historians on this issue. This also gives them the chance to practise examination skills in a summary question.

The rest of the section deals with the human cost of Stalin's programme of modernisation. The text and sources are all geared towards the **Activity** at the end of the section on **page 104**. There is a wealth of information in this section and teachers may well wish to read through the section with pupils before letting them loose on the activity. The aim of the letter is for pupils to make use of the information they have collected in a focused and structured way. Alternatively, they could produce a written response to the key question of the activity, drawing on their findings from previous activities and Focus Tasks.

Modernising agriculture: Collectivisation

This is another major theme of Stalin's time in charge of the USSR. The theme of transformation again looms large as does the plight of the Soviet people. **Questions 1–3** on **page 105** could be usefully tackled as written exercises which will give pupils a target while they read the narrative section on Stalin's agrarian policies. Question 3 raises possibilities for discussion as well.

Questions 4 and 5 on page 105 guide pupils towards analysing a source within its context. Pupils would benefit from a short discussion based on these two questions followed by writing up their findings from their discussions. The **Focus Task** on **page 105** asks pupils to assess different aspects of collectivisation and industrialisation.

Stalin's USSR

This final section of the chapter looks at the nature of life in Stalin's USSR. **Questions 1–3** focus on the source materials and ask pupils to draw conclusions from them by using the context of the narrative text in the section. Pupils should read the questions, then the text, then the sources. The **Focus Task** on **page 107** addresses the thorny issue of why Stalin launched the Purges. Pupils could draw up their own grid to assess the evidence. For weaker pupils, teachers may wish to provide a framework for their answers to the question. A suitable structure might be:

It could be argued that Stalin was trying to remove opposition. The evidence to support this is:

- _____

- _____

- _____

- _____

Another argument is that Stalin was much too afraid of opposition and the Purges were a huge mistake. The evidence to support this is:

- _____

- _____

- _____

- _____

The final **Focus Tasks** on **page 108** attempt to bring all of pupils' work on Stalin together. The general question as to whether Stalin was a success or failure is designed to be executed as a class debate. Pupils might go back to their work on **Worksheet 4.4** and, working in groups, add an additional column for Stalin's rule. The other Focus Task asks pupils to amass evidence of the different methods of control employed by Stalin.

WORKSHEET

4.1

Russia, the Tsar and the people 1900–1917

Tsar Nicholas II was at the centre of Russia's history from 1900 until he was killed in 1918. Use the table below to note down key events, decisions and information about the relationship between the Tsar and his people.

When you have completed the table, it should be a useful summary of the Tsar's rule. This should also be a helpful revision aid.

AIM

To chart the relationship between the Tsar and the Russian people, 1900–1917

RESOURCES

	Tsar's system of government	Tsar's popularity with ordinary people	Tsar's popularity with the aristocracy and middle classes	Important decisions made by the Tsar in this period	Your view of these decisions	Other important events affecting the Tsar
1900–1904						
1905–1906						
1906–1914						
1914–1916						
1917						

WORKSHEET
4.2
Russia 1903 – a status report

AIM

To show understanding of the state of Russia in 1903

RESOURCES

To: His Majesty Tsar Nicholas II, Emperor of All The Russias
From: Your loyal but worried minister

Your Majesty

I feel that I must submit this report in order to warn you about the state of your country. I am first of all concerned about your government because:

- _____
- _____
- _____

You should also be concerned about the peasants in Russia. Although they are loyal to you they suffer badly:

- _____
- _____
- _____

Russia is not a fair society. There are great differences between rich and poor. For example:

- _____
- _____
- _____

The workers in the towns are often no better off than the peasants:

- _____
- _____
- _____

You should also be aware that there are various groups within Russia which oppose you:

- _____
- _____
- _____

EXTENSION WORK

Look back at Sources 2a and 2b (page 77) and other work you have done on Tsar Nicholas so far. Now use examples to explain fully whether you think one of the Tsar's ministers really would write a report like the one you have just written.

How did the Tsar survive the 1905 revolution?

To describe and explain the measures taken by the Tsar from 1905 onwards

Read through pages 80–83 and use the information and sources to complete the boxes below.

How the Tsar crushed the revolution

Government action

Effect

Government action

Effect

Government action

Effect

How the Tsar kept control

Government action

Effect

Government action

Effect

Government action

Effect

Once you have completed the boxes you can use it to plan answers to the following questions. You should aim to answer them in about 100–150 words.

1 'The Tsar survived the 1905 revolution more because his opponents were ineffective than because he acted effectively himself.' Do the sources and your own knowledge of the 1905 revolution support this view?

Divide your answer into sections:
i The Tsar's opponents; how they opposed the Tsar; whether they were well organised and effective; whether they worked well together.
ii The Tsar's actions; how he dealt with the revolutionaries in the early stages of the revolution; how he bought time; how he defeated the rebels.

2 'Only the work of Stolypin, his minister, enabled the Tsar to avoid another revolution after 1905.' Do the sources and your own knowledge of the period 1906–1914 support this view?

Divide your answer into sections again:
i Stolypin's land reforms and their effects on the peasants
ii Stolypin's attitude to protesters
iii Whether Stolypin removed discontent with the Tsar's rule
iv Events after Stolypin's death

WORKSHEET

How well was Russia governed 1900–1941?

4.4

AIM

To test the performance of Russia's government over a long period

RESOURCES

What makes a good government? In the table below is a list of what a Russian might expect from their governments in the period 1900–1941. First look back through your work on Russia so far and decide whether or not Russia had a good government from 1900 to 1914. Later you will be able to fill in the columns on the Bolsheviks and Stalin to give your opinions on how well *they* governed Russia.

	Example of Tsar's government trying to do this	Example of Bolsheviks trying to do this	Example of Stalin trying to do this	Extent of success or failure on a scale of 1–5 (1 = total failure, 5 = complete success)		
				Tsar	Bolshe-viks	Stalin
Trying to improve the lives of all its people						
Building up agriculture and industry						
Listening and responding to the population						
Running the country efficiently						
Defending the country from its enemies						

EXTENSION WORK

In a small group look over your completed table and compare your results with others.
• **Decide which government actions were failures or successes.**
• **For the failures, suggest how they could have been avoided or handled better.**

How did the First World War weaken the Tsar's government?

AIM

To explain the impact of the First World War on Russia

RESOURCES

Use Sources 19 and 21–24 and the text on pages 84–85 to investigate the impact of the First World War on Russia. Work in four stages.

Stage 1: Look only at the statistical sources (Sources 21–23). Write down what they reveal about:
a) conditions in Russia
b) how these weakened the Tsar's position.

Stage 2: Now look at the written sources (Sources 19, 20 and 24). Write down what they reveal about:
a) the running of the war and government
b) how this weakened the Tsar's position.

Stage 3: Now read through the information in the text and find examples which:
a) back up the story told by the statistical sources
b) back up the story told by the written sources.

Stage 4: Make a note of any other factors which you come across.

EXTENSION WORK

Now use your work to write an essay of about 200–250 words with the title 'How did the First World War weaken the Tsar's government?'.

You could begin your essay with the following paragraph:

The First World War had a disastrous impact on Russia and badly weakened the Tsar's hold on his country. Statistics from the time suggest that conditions in Russia were very bad, and were desperate by 1914. For example:

* _____

* _____

* _____

The story told by these statistics is backed up by

* _____

* _____

* _____

WORKSHEET

4.6a

Why did the Tsarist regime collapse in 1917?

AIM

To explain the relative importance of different causes of the collapse of the regime

RESOURCES

The diagram below shows five important reasons for the collapse of the Tsarist system in 1917. However, it does not suggest how these causes were linked to each other. Your task is to draw lines between these factors to show that you think there is a connection between them.

You must be able to justify the lines that you have drawn. After you have made the connections, label each of your lines with a number and complete the boxes underneath the diagram.

Failures in the war

Strikes

Food shortages

The mutiny in the army

The Tsarina and Rasputin

Line _____
connects: _____
and _____
Explanation: _____
_____
_____

Line _____
connects: _____
and _____
Explanation: _____
_____
_____

Line _____
connects: _____
and _____
Explanation: _____
_____
_____

Line _____
connects: _____
and _____
Explanation: _____
_____
_____

WORKSHEET

4.6b

Why did the 1917 revolution succeed when the 1905 revolution failed?

Complete the boxes below as part of a special report on why the 1917 revolution succeeded.

AIM

To explain the relative importance of different causes of the collapse of the regime

RESOURCES

Factor: MUTINY IN THE ARMY

Present in 1905? _____

Present in 1917? _____

Importance in 1917: _____

Factor: FAILURES IN THE WAR

Present in 1905? _____

Present in 1917? _____

Importance in 1917: _____

WHY DID THE 1917 REVOLUTION SUCCEED?

Factor: STRIKES

Present in 1905? _____

Present in 1917? _____

Importance in 1917: _____

Factor: TSARINA AND RASPUTIN

Present in 1905? _____

Present in 1917? _____

Importance in 1917: _____

Factor: FOOD SHORTAGES

Present in 1905? _____

Present in 1917? _____

Importance in 1917: _____

How effective was the Provisional Government?

AIM

To assess how well the Provisional Government ran Russia

RESOURCES

1 Use the information and sources on pages 86–87 to complete this chart.

2 a) In the final columns add your own grade, and suggestions for improvement.

  b) At the bottom write your own overall assessment of their performance.

ANNUAL REPORT ON PROVISIONAL GOVERNMENT				
Area of performance	How the government dealt with it	Result of the government's action	Grade A–G	Suggestions for improvement
The war				
The land question				
Food supplies				
Overall assessment of the Provisional Government's performance				

EXTENSION WORK

Explain which of these two statements you agree with most.

Statement 1 'The Provisional Government was faced with insurmountable problems. It never really had a chance of surviving.'

Statement 2 'The Provisional Government deserved to fail because it never tried to run Russia in the interests of the Russian people.'

Remember to say why you chose either 1 or 2, and why you did not choose the other.

WORKSHEET *Lenin*

4.8

AIM

To explain the importance of Lenin as a factor in the Russian Revolution

RESOURCES

PROFILE

Vladimir Illych Lenin

★ Born 1870 into a respectable Russian family.
★ Brother hanged 1887 for plotting against the Tsar.
★ Graduated from St Petersburg University after being thrown out of Kazan University for his political beliefs.
★ One of the largest Okhrana files was about him!
★ Exiled to Siberia 1897–1900.
★ 1900–1905 lived in various countries writing the revolutionary newspaper *Iskra* ('The Spark').
★ Took part in 1905 revolution but was forced to flee.
★ Returned to Russia after the first revolution in 1917.
★ Led Bolsheviks to power November 1917.

PROFILE

Why Lenin appealed to people

PROFILE

His personal qualities

PROFILE

His strength as a leader

WORKSHEET *Why were the Bolsheviks successful?*

4.9

The other mighty factors

Read the comment below, which is by the historian Robert Service, an expert on this period.

1 Look back over your work on Russia in 1917 and before and write down what you think he means by 'other mighty factors'.

2 Use the boxes to write a short explanation of each one of these factors. You may wish to add a few boxes of your own.

3 Draw lines to show the connections between the factors which you have identified. Make sure you can explain why you have drawn each line.

FACTOR

The [November] Revolution has often and widely been held to have been mainly Lenin's revolution. But was it? Certainly Lenin had a heavier impact on the course than anyone else. The point is, however, that great historical changes are brought about not only by individuals. There were other mighty factors at work as well in Russia in 1917 ... Lenin could simply not have done or even coordinated everything.

FACTOR

FACTOR

FACTOR

FACTOR

FACTOR

FACTOR

Write about 200–250 words to explain why the Bolsheviks were successful in 1917. Use the factors which you have already identified as headings for each paragraph in your answer and remember to explain the connections between events.

WORSHEET

4.10

An inside view of the Russian Revolution

AIM

To examine the experiences of ordinary Russians in the revolutionary period

RESOURCES

Vladimir is a Russian worker living in Petrograd with his wife and three small children. He comes from a large family, but they all live in the countryside. He works in a steel mill and goes back to the family home each summer to help with the harvest. This is now more difficult because of the war, but he tries because two of his brothers are in the army and one other has already been killed. He belongs to a trade union and likes to tell people about the scars he received after he was flogged by the secret police for taking part in a strike in 1912. He is a strong supporter of the Petrograd Soviet but he is not sure about whether he can trust the Bolsheviks or not.

Imagine that you are able to visit Vladimir at different times in the period 1917–1921. Each time you visit him you ask him for his views on the latest developments.
Fill in the table below.

Date	Developments	Vladimir's views
November 1917	How Bolshevik decrees might affect Vladimir (look at Factfile)	
January 1918	Who he might have voted for in Assembly elections and how he might feel about its dissolution	
March 1918	How Vladimir feels about the war and the Treaty of Brest–Litovsk	
The end of 1918	Which side Vladimir supports in the Civil War (and whether he has any choice)	
Early to mid 1921	How Vladimir feels about War Communism	

WORKSHEET
Why did the Bolsheviks win the Civil War?

4.11

Imagine it is the end of the war and you have been asked to make a victory poster for the Bolsheviks celebrating the victory and showing the main reasons for success.

Before you design your poster you will need to do some background research.

AIM

To describe and explain the main reasons for the Bolshevik success

RESOURCES

In this box, decide what images will be in your poster. Think about:

• background (e.g. marching soldiers)
• the central image (e.g. a picture of Lenin)
• how you will show the reasons (pictures? words? both?).

In this box note down all of the reasons why the Bolsheviks won the Civil War. Then lightly cross out those reasons which you think are not suitable for the Soviet people to see.

In this box make a note of what you are trying to achieve with this poster (e.g. to convince people that the Bolsheviks are strong protectors of the people).

Try out different slogans.

EXTENSION WORK

'The Bolshevik victory in the Civil War was a result of the incompetence of the Whites.'
Use the evidence in this section to decide whether you agree with this statement.

WORSHEET

4.12

How did the Bolsheviks consolidate their rule?

AIM

To explain the steps taken by the Bolsheviks to secure their position

RESOURCES

It is January 1924. Lenin is dead. Your task is to look back at the measures he used to consolidate Bolshevik rule.

1 On the timeline below, mark the key events in Russia's history in this period.

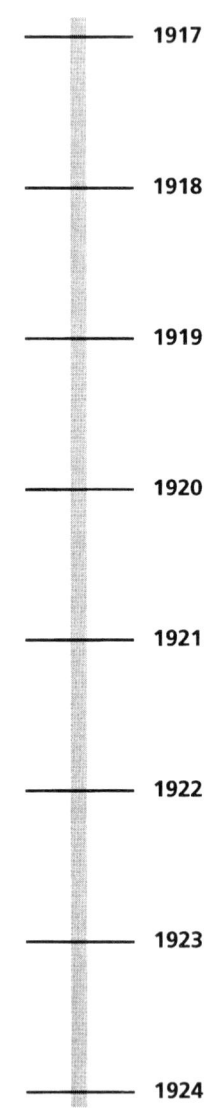

— 1917

— 1918

— 1919

— 1920

— 1921

— 1922

— 1923

— 1924

2 Mark two important points on your timeline:
  i The period when you feel Bolshevik rule faced the greatest threat
  ii The time when you feel Bolshevik rule was most secure.

3 In about 200–250 words, explain how the Bolsheviks made their rule more secure in the period 1917–1924. Organise your answer into five paragraphs:

- The Red Army (role in the revolution, the Civil War)
- Treatment of opponents of Bolsheviks (Cheka, Assembly)
- War Communism (reasons for it, effects on Russia, effects on Bolshevik control)
- The New Economic Policy (reasons for it, effects on Russia, effects on Bolshevik control)
- Your conclusion as to which of the above is the most important factor.

The struggle to succeed Lenin

AIM

To examine the evidence to support different views on Stalin

RESOURCES

In groups, look at the following statements and decide on a scale of 1–5 how far you agree with them.

1 Stalin was a dull and unimaginative politician.
2 Stalin appeared to be a dull and unimaginative politician.
3 Trotsky lost the contest because of his mistakes.
4 Stalin trusted to luck rather than careful planning.
5 Stalin was ruthless and devious.

Read through pages 98–99 and in the table below fill in the evidence to support each statement.

Statement 1	Statement 2	Statement 3	Statement 4	Statement 5

EXTENSION WORK

'Stalin had no imagination and little political ability. His rise to power can only be explained by good luck.'
Write 2–3 paragraphs to explain whether you agree, disagree or partially agree with this statement.

WORKSHEET

Why did Stalin win?

4.14

AIM

To use a range of sources to explain Stalin's victory

RESOURCES

Imagine you have to prepare a radio news feature on the reasons why Stalin, not Trotsky, became Lenin's successor.

Your first task is to plan your broadcast. Radio producers use flow diagrams to plan their broadcasts. Here is a suggested opening for your broadcast. You will then add other sections to it.

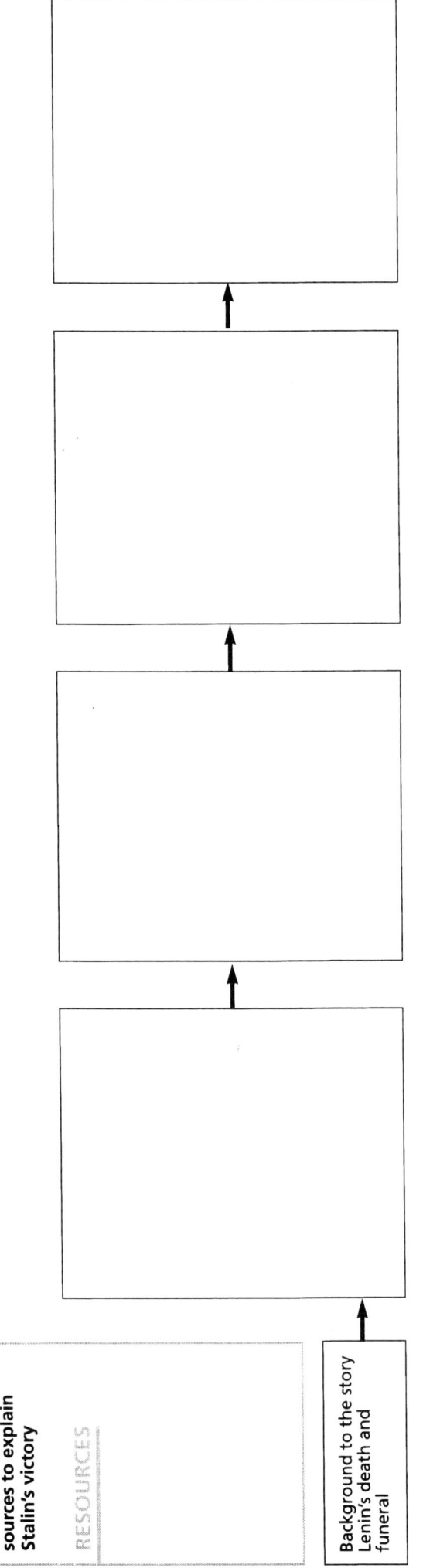

Background to the story
Lenin's death and funeral

You must decide what features go into the rest of your programme, how long they will last and the order in which they will come up. Some of the elements you will need to include are:

- Profiles of the two main contenders. These could be presented as descriptions by people who knew them.
- Interviews with the key figures in the leadership contest about their aims. These aims could be summarised as slogans.
- A story element telling listeners about the key events in the struggle.
- A conclusion on why Stalin was successful.

WORKSHEET

Why did Stalin introduce the Five-Year Plans?

4.15

AIM

To investigate why Stalin tried to modernise the USSR

RESOURCES

As Stalin announced his Five-Year Plans to the USSR, many observers in western Europe were wondering what his plans were really all about. Was he really trying to build a better Russia or was he preparing the USSR for war?

Using the information and sources on page 100 investigate what Stalin's motives really were in launching the Five-Year Plans.

The table below should help you organise your thoughts.

Source/information	Supports the idea of Five-Year Plans as a security measure?	Supports the idea that the Five-Year Plans were to improve the lives of the people of the USSR?	Value/reliability of source for this investigation

In pairs or small groups decide why you think Stalin launched the Five-Year Plans and then draw up two lists:

• One (top secret to be found in Stalin's safe) with the true aims of the Five-Year Plans
• Another list of the aims of the Plans to be handed out to foreign journalists and governments.

WORKSHEET

4.16 *Were the Five-Year Plans successful?*

AIM

To use a range of sources to evaluate the success of the Five-Year Plans

RESOURCES

Study Sources 6–12 on pages 101–102 carefully.

1 What is the message of Source 11?

2 How could Stalin use Sources 7 and 8 to support the claims made in Source 11?

3 Compare Sources 6 and 10. Do they agree or disagree about the Five-Year Plans? Explain your answer.

4 'Historians find it difficult to make a judgement on whether the Five-Year Plans were a success because the evidence is confusing and unreliable.' Do Sources 6–12 support this statement? Use the following framework to help you answer this question.

Sources 6–12 represent a wide range of different types of sources.

For instance Sources 7–9 are all statistical sources. They give the impression that . . .

. . . .

However, it may not be wise to make a judgement only on these sources because . . .

. . . .

Sources 6, 11 and 12 come from the time of the Five-Year Plans. They seem to indicate that . . .

. . . .

However, this can often mean that the information is less reliable or is even a form of propaganda. For instance . . .

. . . .

Finally, Source 10 is a piece of secondary source material. This has advantages and disadvantages . . .

. . . .

Conclusion

Taken as a whole, the evidence in Sources 6–12 presents a picture which is . . .

. . . .

I therefore feel that the statement is _____ because . . .

. . . .

5 *Germany 1918–1945*

Key features of the chapter

Element	Issue(s) covered	Concepts and skills	Format(s) for pupil work
Focus Task (p.110): Germany 1919	Range of problems facing Germany and new government	Key features of historical situation	Research, prioritising, presentation in chart
Focus Task (p.115): Hyperinflation	Did Treaty cause hyperinflation?	Causes, interpretations and deploying knowledge	Formal questions and extended writing based on synthesis of sources
Focus Task (p.116): Weimar Germany	How far did Weimar Republic recover in the 1920s?	Use of sources, historical interpretations	Research, organising into table, extended writing
Activity (p.117): Hitler and Nazis, 1923	Hitler's views and early ideas	Deploying knowledge, use of sources, features of historical situation	Research, synthesising sources and text into a profile
Focus Task (p.118): Nazis in 1923	What Nazism stood for	Deploying knowledge, use of sources, features of historical situation	Research, synthesising sources and text into a profile
Focus Task (p.119): Nazism, 1926	Nazism 1926 compared with in 1923	Knowledge, study of change, use of sources	Comparison
Focus Task (p.123): 1933	How did Hitler become Chancellor?	Deployment of knowledge, features of historical situation, interpretation	Research, synthesising sources and text – follow-up extended writing
Focus Task (p.127): Police state	Elements of Nazi police state	Selecting and deploying knowledge	Deploying key points into table format
Focus Task (p.131): Nazi Germany	How did Nazis control Germany?	Use of sources, deploying knowledge, interpretations	Discussion, possibility of follow-up essay
Focus Task (p.135): Nazis and young people	How did young people react to Nazi regime?	Deploying knowledge, using sources in context	Substantiated answers to question
Focus Task (p.135): Nazis and women	Success of Nazi policies towards women	Use of sources, features of an historical situation	Testing contrasting hypotheses with evidence
Focus Task (p.137): Hitler's Germany	Assessment of historian's views	Interpretations, use of sources, key features	Investigation of validity of historian's viewpoint
Focus Task (p.139): Wartime Germany	How war changed Germany	Change, key features, deploying knowledge	Table leading to written report
Activity (p.140): Wartime propaganda	Analysing propaganda	Study of change, use of sources	Analysis of sources using context
Focus Task (p.144): Germany under Nazis	Was Nazi Germany a totalitarian state?	Deploying knowledge, use of sources, interpretations	Substantiated answers to key questions

Part 1 THE WEIMAR REPUBLIC AND THE RISE OF THE NAZIS

The impact of the First World War – the Issue Starter

The issue starter in this chapter is a short examination of how, by 1919, the mighty had fallen. Pupils who have studied World War I will be familiar with the Kaiser and his views and eccentricities, otherwise a little background will be necessary. The essential point for pupils to grasp is the might and splendour of Germany in 1914 and the contrast with its condition in 1919. The best demonstration of this humbling fall will be found in Sources 1 and 2. As pupils work through this section, you could throw in some helpful whole-class discussion questions:

- Find six words to describe the condition of Germany – three for 1914, three for 1918.
- The Kaiser fled in 1918 – do you think Germans blamed him for their plight?
- Would they still blame the Kaiser in 1923, or the government which replaced him?

Germany 1917–1929

The aim of this section is simply to chronicle the changeover from predominantly autocratic to democratic government. The key point for teachers to stress is that while British people of the 1990s will naturally distrust autocracy, Germans in 1919 felt much the same way about democracy. This unease can only have been heightened by the chaotic state of the country at the end of the war. To most Germans, such a situation must have seemed to be crying out for firm government.

The Focus Task on page 110 asks pupils to turn the information in Source 4 into a summary diagram. **Worksheet 5.1** provides a framework for this and some extension work as well.

Revolts and rebellions 1919–1923

This section is crucial in establishing in pupils' minds the concept of a country in almost complete chaos. **Question 1** on **page 111** and **questions 1 and 2** on **page 112** are 'intermediary' questions, aimed simply at reinforcing important factual points. The first question directs pupils to the fact that all of the rebel factions of the period were well armed. Indeed Germany after the war was awash with weapons.

Questions 1 and 2 on page 112 might be attempted profitably as written exercises. Pupils need to see the extent of the hurt caused by the Treaty. This might be reinforced by reminding them of the pride and majesty of Germany in 1914 as described in the issue starter. **Question 3** on **page 112** is also important. Along with the previous question, it establishes in pupils' minds the essential strength of the Right in Germany despite the large popular support for the left-wing parties.

Economic disaster

As well as dealing with what is in itself a spectacular topic, this section builds on the sense of disillusionment with democracy established in the previous section. **Questions 4–6** on **page 113** are again intermediary questions, most effectively used as small-group or class discussion questions.

Question 4 employs the principles for using visuals established on page 50 of this book, looking at:

- context of the source – concurrent events and issues
- background
- figures – size, position, expression
- captions
- words spoken by characters.

Question 5 (page 113) is a simple cross-referencing exercise, but leads on to question 6 which raises an important issue. This could be addressed in discussion, but Worksheet 5.2 offers an extension activity designed to improve pupils' understanding of a key issue.

Questions 1–4 on pages 114–115 could be used as discussion or written exercises. The emphasis throughout is on pupils integrating sources, cross referencing and synthesising their findings. Question 2 is crucial in this respect. Questions 3 and 4 ask pupils to use the source materials in their context to show their understanding of the issues. The key process is, of course, the explanation of their choice rather than the choice itself.

The Focus Task on page 115 practises similar skills, again demanding a use of source material in context. Parts 1 and 2 are source-analysis exercises. For part 3 pupils could be challenged by first having to establish a character and viewpoint for the writer and then making sure that their answer is consistent with this. More able pupils might try this with several characters. A Spartacist and a Freikorps veteran might reach the same conclusion for very different reasons. Part 4 might lead to a simple judgement or could involve pupils answering the question in several paragraphs. They might find the framework on Worksheet 5.3 helpful.

The Weimar Republic under Stresemann

A number of key points emerge in this section, and pupils need to be made aware of them. The relationship between Stresemann's success and Nazi frustrations in this period is well understood. However, pupils need to be reminded of Stresemann's own right-wing credentials, which speak volumes about where power lay in Germany. This could be addressed orally through a careful reading of the text and study of Source 22. Similarly, the underlying weaknesses of the Weimar structure are well illustrated in Source 22, addressed by question 1 on page 118.

The Focus Task on page 116 pulls all of these issues together. By drawing up and using a table such as the one below pupils will be better able to gain an overview of the topic.

	Stresemann	Egbert
Political views		
Problems faced		
Support in Germany		
Support from outside Germany		

Additionally, the table format is a powerful barrier against copying – pupils need to be selective.

Hitler and the Nazis

The sense of fragile stability established in the previous section provides the foundation for this next section. The Activity on page 117 asks pupils to use the text and sources together (in context) to chart Hitler's rise to prominence within the Nazi Party and within Germany. The bullet point prompts provide a structure for the article and pupils should sift the evidence to pull out key points about Hitler. For greater rigour, teachers may wish to set word limits to discourage copying, or insist on at least one quotation.

Worksheet 5.4 sets out a plan of action for pupils to plan and write the article. The **Focus Task** on **page 118** follows a similar pattern. Pupils might be given a time limit for the speech to ensure that they process the information rather than simply move it from the book to their own files. Weaker pupils might need to be directed to the sources and sections of text which relate to specific bullet points (e.g. Weimar Constitution referred to in Source 28 and under the Munich Putsch heading).

The follow-up **Focus Task** on **page 119** could be supported similarly, and pupils referred particularly to *Mein Kampf*. They could use the same bullet point headings and simply indicate what changes, if any, have taken place.

The Depression and the rise of the Nazis

This section targets two key areas. Firstly, pupils must appreciate the impact of the Depression, coming as it did after prosperity, but before memories of the inflation had faded. Secondly, they must grasp that although the Depression made it possible, the Nazis' rise to prominence was due to their exploiting its effects. This can be illustrated by looking at Sources 30 and 31 together.

The text and sources are geared towards the demanding **Activity** on **page 121**. The aim is for pupils to assess the reasons for the contrast in the Nazis' fortunes between 1923 and 1933. Again, the task can be customised for different pupils with such devices as word limits, restrictions to particular source material, the inclusion of visual sources and guidance on depth of investigation. **Worksheet 5.5a** provides a framework for the task. **Worksheet 5.5b** provides an alternative recording format suitable for less able pupils. (Please note that the text shown on Source 38 has been translated into English.)

How did Hitler become Chancellor in 1933?

From the scene setting of the first section on the rise of the Nazis, this next section recounts Hitler's ascension to the position of Chancellor. The focus of the section is very much on the failings of the Weimar system, but also points to the lack of will all round to make the system work.

The major **Focus Task** on **page 123** attempts to pull together this issue and a number of issues from previous sections. **Worksheet 5.6** provides support and guidance on this challenging task. For parts 1 and 2, pupils could annotate the actual sheet or draw up a table for their views. The comparison of marks out of 10 is intended to be a stimulus for fruitful discussion, in which pupils must substantiate the points they make. Part 3 is designed to encourage pupils to produce a structured, coherent piece of extended writing.

Part 2 **HITLER'S GERMANY**

Hitler's dictatorship

In this section pupils will see how Hitler consolidated his position and began to carry out the Nazi revolution in Germany. Although important in itself, the section will also give pupils a vital perspective on later events and issues. The information here is indispensable if pupils are to address successfully questions such as:

• Was Germany a totalitarian state?
• How far was Hitler alone in control and responsible?
• Why was opposition so unsuccessful?

Questions 1–4 on page 124–125 raise some important issues. Questions 1 and 2 are worth written answers, not least because they pull narrative and source material together. Questions 3 and 4 are more reflective and are best dealt with orally.

The Nazi police state 1933–1945

Pupils should have no difficulty making the links between this section and the preceding one. The **Focus Task** on **page 127** concentrates on the Nazis' instruments of control from 1933 to 1945. The success of that control is considered later and so the task simply asks pupils to record the features of the police state. Headings are suggested for a table and the second part of the question should help pupils to process the information. **Worksheet 5.7** contains a recording format.

Opposition to the Nazis

This section is short but extremely important, in that it illuminates the efficiency of the mechanism of the police state. The four questions ask pupils to read the text carefully and draw conclusions from it.

The culture of Nazi Germany

This key section builds on the previous sections and culminates in pupils discussing whether persuasion and indoctrination were more important factors than intimidation and repression. **Question 5** on **page 129** asks pupils to make judgements from photographic sources on the Nuremberg rallies. Many pupils find photographs difficult to interrogate and the aim of this exercise is to encourage them to make the source useful by identifying its context.

Similarly, **questions 1 and 3** on **pages 130 and 131** ask pupils to deal with challenging sources and contexts. **Source 16** is a difficult source, but once its context is understood its message becomes much clearer. In **question 2**, giving a definition of propaganda should be distinguished from giving a mere example.

Questions 4–7 on page 131 explore propaganda further. These questions are suitable for class or small-group discussion although a formal written format would also work. The ideas and concepts raised by these questions feed into the Activity and the Focus Task on **page 131**.

The **Activity** on Josef Goebbels clearly focuses upon the role of an individual. Pupils will profit from looking at profiles of figures such as Lenin, Hitler and Mao Tse-tung to get the feel of the task. The focus of the activity is on the impact of Goebbels and his importance to the Nazi regime. The point should be stressed that the information in the profile is starter information and the pupils' task is to add to it.

The **Focus Task** is supported by **Worksheet 5.8**. The aim is for pupils to select and deploy evidence which supports each of the statements. The linked circles help pupils to visualise the sophisticated concept of interlinked events and issues.

How did the Nazis deal with young people?

This is an important but also particularly fascinating section for most pupils since they have a true vantage point of experience from which to make comparisons. The questions on **pages 131–133** are well suited to individual written answers but pupils will gain much from answering these questions collaboratively. The questions demand that pupils assess the sources in the context of the accompanying narrative, and as such they practise a valuable skill.

The Activity on page 133 can assess the extent to which pupils have truly grasped the issues under study. The creation of a poster is in no way a soft option, and this needs to be stressed. Firstly, pupils who cannot draw can put together a detailed brief for an artist with rough sketches. The poster contains some important aspects of history. For the poster aimed at young people, there are a number of criteria to be met:

- What images, words and associations will attract young people? (Look at modern magazines – the Nazis were masters of PR and many of their ideas are still used.)
- What messages are to be sent to young people (e.g. on race, militarism, fitness, obedience)?
- Do they want to include negative factors (e.g. Jews, Communists)?

    For their parents, pupils must consider:
- How the message is sold to parents (e.g. health, education, obedience)
- What might be hidden from parents.

Did all young people support the Nazis?

This section is important in that it draws pupils towards questioning the extent to which the Nazi state was a monolith. The descriptions of the Swing movement and the Edelweiss Pirates should maintain the interest of pupils without much difficulty. Indeed, the section on the Edelweiss Pirates offers much opportunity for thoughtful self-reflection and also for pupils to empathise with those living today under the shadow of repressive regimes (e.g. in Iraq).

    The main concern of the **Focus Task** at the top of **page 135** is to establish an overview of Nazi youth policy. The questions and activities up to this point should provide the raw material from which a structured written answer to the question can be put together. **Worksheet 5.9** provides a framework for the answer.

Women in Nazi Germany

This section is directed very clearly at the **Focus Task** at the bottom of **page 135**. Pupils can use the two statements as headings and draw up for and against columns as they sift for evidence and examples for each section. From this research they could then present a paragraph summarising their conclusions.

Did Germans gain from Nazi rule?

The section on women points to the rather mixed blessings of Nazism, even for 'good Aryans'. This section explores the notion further. The **Focus Task** on **page 137** asks pupils to give their reactions to a statement by the British historian George Clare.

Worksheet 5.10 sets out a way in which pupils could personalise the task and then 'zoom out' to make a judgement based on a wider perspective.

The impact of the Second World War on Germany

This long and detailed section provides a stark contrast to the previous one. The inexorable defeat and the impact of the bombing should enable pupils to understand readily why support for the regime began to waver. **Question 1** on **page 139** should provide for interesting discussion on bombing, with the possibility of broadening discussion into the morality of such tactics.

The Focus Task on page 139 is supported by **Worksheet 5.11**. Pupils will need to read the text carefully to decide which events should go on the timeline and in what order. Some may benefit from being provided with key points to 'slot into' their timeline such as:

Sept 1939 War begins
1939–1941 Spectacular successes
1941 Hitler attacks USSR
1942–1943 German army begins to suffer against USSR
1944 Tide turns against Germany – retreating vs Russians and D-Day invasions in France
1945 Defeat

The Activity on page 140 focuses pupils back on Goebbels' attempts to maintain support and control with propaganda measures. Pupils can analyse the features of the sources, but the key to an effective analysis is their understanding of the context.

The persecution of the Jews and other minorities

This detailed section sets out the progression of events from Hitler's anti-Semitic beliefs through to the grim details of the Final Solution. **Questions 1 and 2** on **page 142** ask pupils to view a number of sources critically and to evaluate whether they give a clear picture of Kristallnacht. These should be tackled as a written exercise, and of course a satisfactory answer must consider these sources in context. **Question 3** takes the issue of context a step further in that pupils must integrate their findings from this section with their work on propaganda and the Nazi police state.

The Jewish butcher in **Source 45** is mincing a rat below a sign reading 'Mince – very cheap today'.

The Final Solution

This final and sombre section rounds off the study of Germany with a **Focus Task** which addresses the issue of whether Nazi Germany was truly a totalitarian state. Part 1, the definition of totalitarianism, could spark some fruitful discussion, particularly if pupils have studied the USSR. Parts 2 and 3 require reasoned and structured answers.

Parts 4 and 5 are rather more open and address issues beyond the scope of GCSE History. **Worksheet 5.12** contains a framework in which pupils could formalise the debate, particularly about question 4.

WORSHEET

5.1

What state was Germany in at the end of the War?

AIM

To record the problems faced by Germany in 1919

RESOURCES

Using the text and sources on pages 109 and 110 complete the diagram below.
One example has been done for you.

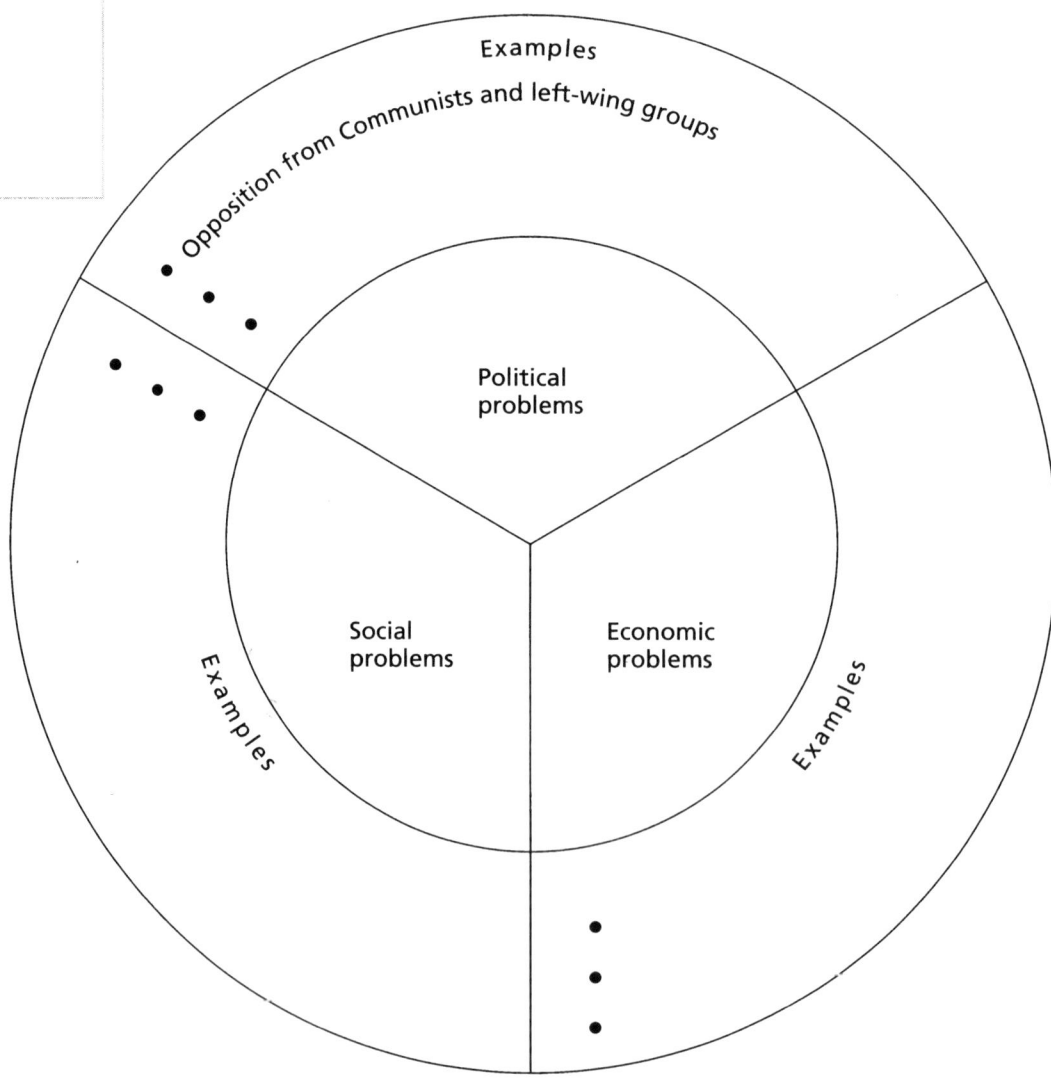

Examples

Opposition from Communists and left-wing groups

Political
problems

Social
problems

Economic
problems

Examples

Examples

EXTENSION WORK

1 Re-draw the diagram with the same segments but do not draw them all the same size. Decide which problem you think is the most serious and make that the largest. The smallest problem should have the smallest segment.

2 Write a report to explain how your diagram has changed from the original. For each segment explain:
   • **how it has changed**
   • **why you changed it.**

WORKSHEET

5.2

Reparations – the evidence

AIM

To use a range of sources to examine differing views on reparations

RESOURCES

Is it possible to answer the question 'Could Germany afford the reparations payments?' with a simple yes or no answer?

The difficulty with answering the question with 'yes' or 'no' is that the evidence does not all indicate the same answer. There are several different sources of evidence for this issue.

Firstly there is … (type of evidence)

_____

_____

Secondly there is … (type of evidence)

_____

_____

There is also … (type of evidence)

_____

_____

The picture presented by this evidence is confusing as many sources disagree with each other. For example:

Sources ……………… suggest …

_____

_____

whereas Sources ……………… suggest …

_____

_____

Therefore, in conclusion, I believe …

_____

_____

_____

_____

_____

_____

_____

_____

_____

WORKSHEET

5.3

Who or what would you blame for hyperinflation?

AIM

To evaluate causes of hyperinflation

RESOURCES

Germans blamed hyperinflation on the Treaty of Versailles. Let's call this **Cause 1**.

However, as well as the treaty there are other possible causes:

Cause 2 The disruption caused by revolutions
Cause 3 The government printing too much money
Cause 4 War damage
Cause 5 France's actions

Look back over pages 110–114 and complete the table below listing all the evidence.
Make sure you use the text and the sources.

Cause 1	Cause 2	Cause 3	Cause 4	Cause 5

Once you have completed the evidence table,

EITHER
a) Choose the one cause which you believe was the most important. Describe your cause fully and explain why you have chosen it.
OR
b) Choose three of the causes which you believe to be linked and explain how they are linked.

WORSHEET 5.4 *A new force on the political scene?*

AIM

To examine Hitler and the early Nazis, using sources to determine the key factors which allowed him to rise to prominence

RESOURCES

Use the information and sources on pages 113–117 to write a newspaper article about the rise of Hitler and the Nazi Party.

In recent months a new force seems to be arising in German politics. Adolf Hitler and the Nazis have hit the headlines with their meetings, banners and radical ideas. What makes this man successful?

HITLER'S BACKGROUND

BELIEFS

QUALITIES

Hitler and the Nazis, 1933

AIM

To examine the factors involved in Hitler's rise to power and the popularity of the Nazis by 1933

RESOURCES

On Worksheet 5.4 you wrote about Hitler and the Nazis in 1923. It is now 1933. You have to write an article to explain what has changed since then.

Ten years ago it hardly seemed possible that the Nazi Party and Hitler could so dominate German politics. What has made the Nazis so popular?

Choose which picture of Hitler would best illustrate this article.

HOW THE FAILURE OF THE MUNICH PUTSCH CHANGED NAZI TACTICS

HOW THE DEPRESSION HAS HELPED THE NAZIS

HOW THE NAZIS HAVE SUCCEEDED IN ELECTIONS

WORSHEET

5.5b

Hitler and the Nazis, 1933

AIM

To explain the impact of various factors on Hitler's rise to power

RESOURCES

Use this sheet for your report.

In each of the boxes, explain how this factor helped Hitler in 1933. If you have space, you could add a picture or diagram.

Nazi policies
helped Hitler...

Nazi campaigns
helped Hitler...

The impact of the Depression
helped Hitler...

HITLER'S RISE IN 1933

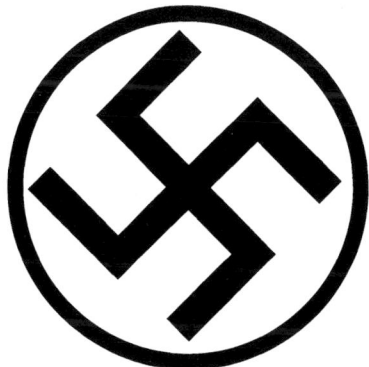

Failures of the Weimar system
helped Hitler...

Other factors
helped Hitler...

WORSHEET

5.6

How did Hitler become Chancellor in 1933?

AIM

To describe and explain how Hitler became Chancellor and to evaluate the relative importance of different causes

RESOURCES

Factors which helped Hitler come to power

1 Nazi strengths	
1.1 Hitler's speaking skills	
1.2 Propaganda campaigns	
1.3 Violent treatment of opposition	
1.4 Criticisms of Weimar system of government	
1.5 Nazi policies	
1.6 Support from big business	

3 Other factors	
3.1 Weaknesses of Weimar Republic	
3.2 Scheming of Hindenburg and von Papen	
3.3 Impact of the Depression	
3.4 Treaty of Versailles	
3.5 Memories of the problems of 1923	

2 Opposition weakness	
2.1 Failure to deal with Depression	
2.2 Failure to co-operate with each other	
2.3 Attitudes of Germans to democratic parties	

Look carefully at each of the factors in the diagram.

1 For each factor, give one example to explain how that factor helped Hitler.
2 Give each factor a mark out of 10 for its importance in bringing Hitler to power. Compare your marks with a partner.
3 Choose what you believe are the five most important factors and write a short paragraph on each. Each paragraph should include:

- an explanation of why you have chosen it
- whether Hitler could have succeeded without this factor
- whether the factor was present in the 1920s and, if it was, why the Nazis did not succeed then.

WORKSHEET

5.7

The Nazi police state

Use the information on pages 126–127 to complete the diagram below.

AIM

To research and describe the key features of the Nazi police state

RESOURCES

The SS

Controlled by: _____

Duties: _____

Methods: _____

How it helped Hitler secure his position:
_____
_____

The Police and the courts

Controlled by: _____

Duties: _____

Methods: _____

How they helped Hitler secure his position:
_____
_____

Concentration camps

Controlled by: _____

Duties: _____

Methods: _____

How they helped Hitler secure his position:
_____
_____

The Gestapo

Controlled by: _____

Duties: _____

Methods: _____

How it helped Hitler secure his position:
_____
_____

How did the Nazis control Germany?

AIM

To compare the relative importance of the different methods of control used by the Nazis

RESOURCES

In groups you are going to discuss which of these three statements you most agree with:

A Goebbels' work was more important to Nazi success than that of Himmler.
B Himmler's work was more important to Nazi success than Goebbels'.
C The techniques of repression and propaganda go hand in hand – neither could work without the other.

How to work

To help you prepare for the group discussion, read pages 128–131. In the diagram below, note down relevant information about each person's work and the links between them.

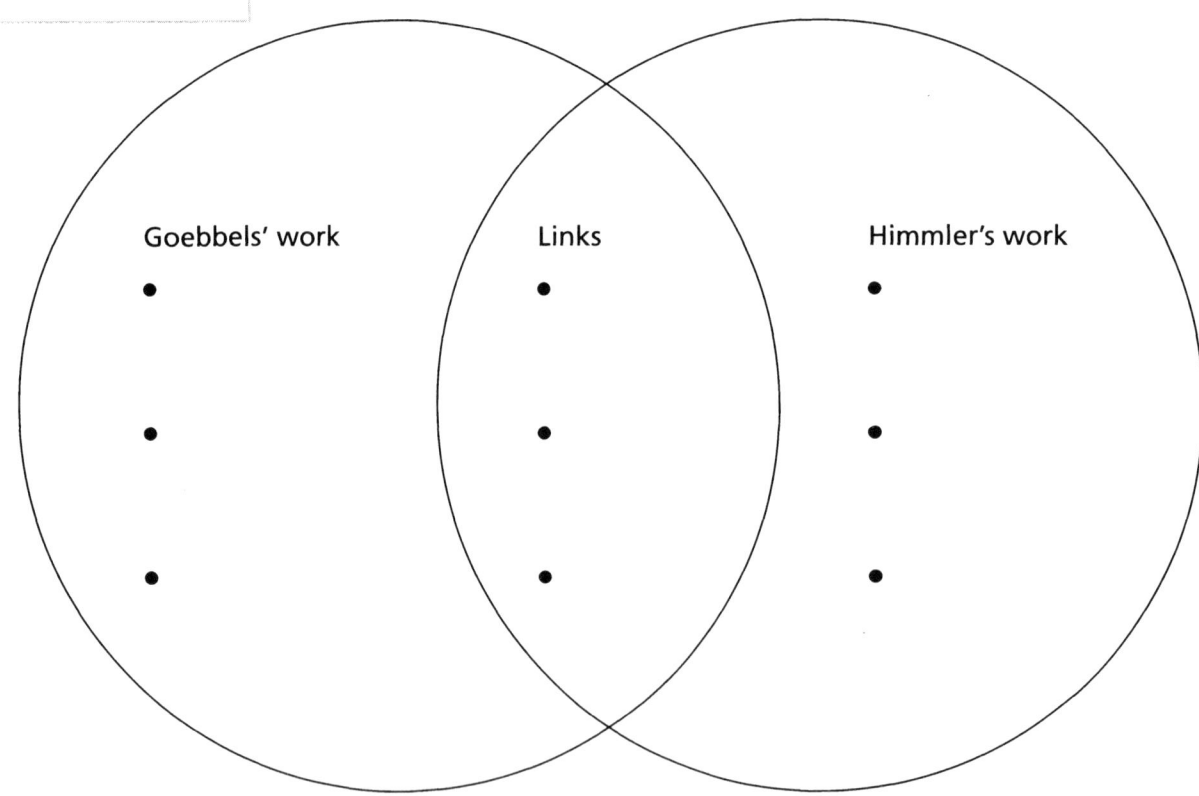

Goebbels' work
•

•

•

Links
•

•

•

Himmler's work
•

•

•

EXTENSION WORK

Write an essay with the title 'How did the Nazis control Germany?'.
• Use either A, B or C as your main line of argument.
• Remember to say what evidence convinces you that A, B or C is the strongest view.
• Also explain whether the two views you reject have any supporting evidence, and why you rejected them.

WORKSHEET

5.9

How did young people react to the Nazi regime?

AIM

To describe and explain the key features of Nazi youth policy and the ways in which young people reacted to that policy

RESOURCES

Young people were among the most fanatical supporters of the Nazi regime and the Nazis had great success in controlling them.

The Nazis wanted to control young people because:

* _____
* _____
* _____

The Nazis used a range of methods to control young people:

* _____
* _____
* _____

However, many young people in Germany were enthusiastic about life under the Nazi regime. They enjoyed:

* _____
* _____
* _____

Not all young people supported the regime, however. Groups which opposed the Nazis were:

* _____
* _____
* _____

They opposed the Nazis because:

* _____
* _____
* _____

Because of their opposition, the Nazis acted against them by:

* _____
* _____

Did Germans gain from Nazi rule?

GCSE Modern World History

AIM

To examine and evaluate different interpretations of life in Nazi Germany

RESOURCES

Think about this issue from the point of view of Heinrich Werner, aged 45, a German worker unemployed from 1929 to 1933 and desperate. He and his family also suffered in the inflation of 1923. He joined the Nazis in 1930.

Read through pages 136–137 and fill in the table.

Aspects of Nazi Germany Heinrich might approve of	Aspects he might dislike but be prepared to ignore	Aspects he might protest about

Now repeat the process for Johann Sturm, a prosperous businessman.

Aspects of Nazi Germany Johann might approve of	Aspects he might dislike but be prepared to ignore	Aspects he might protest about

WORKSHEET

How did the war change life in Germany?

5.11

Look back at pages 137–139.

1 On the left-hand side of the timeline below, fill in some of the key events which show how the war was going for Germany's army.
2 On the right-hand side, show how the war affected German civilians at different times.
3 Choose the one change from the right-hand side which you think had the greatest impact on ordinary Germans and explain your choice.

ARMY   **CIVILIANS**

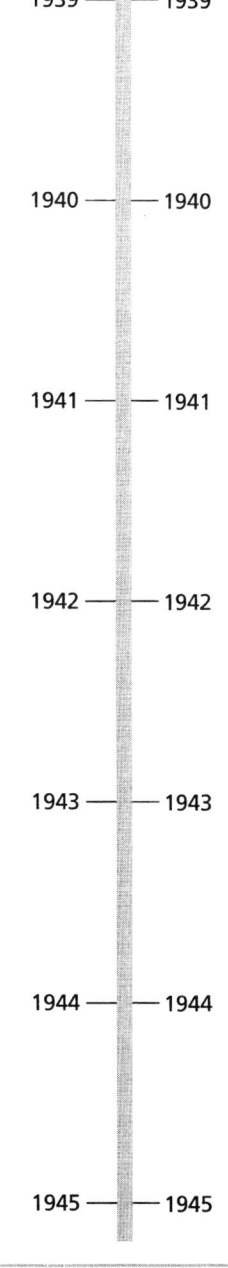

1939 —|— 1939

1940 —|— 1940

1941 —|— 1941

1942 —|— 1942

1943 —|— 1943

1944 —|— 1944

1945 —|— 1945

EXTENSION WORK

Look back at one of the characters you studied in Worksheet 5.10. Describe in about 200 words how the war might have affected him and how his attitudes may have changed.

Was Germany a totalitarian state?

AIM

To use a range of sources and evidence to present a case on whether Nazi Germany really was a totalitarian state

RESOURCES

The scenario

It is 1945 and your group is a team of investigative lawyers at the Nuremberg War Crimes Trials. Your superiors are trying the Nazi leaders like Göring, but your task is to investigate some of the guards at the concentration camp.

The issue

The lawyer representing these guards has argued that the guards were simply obeying orders. In a totalitarian state they had no choice.

Your task

Look back over your work on Nazi Germany and especially at pages 141–143. You must decide how to respond to the defence of these guards that they were simply obeying orders.

You should present a report of around 200 words explaining why you feel these men should or should not stand trial. The issues you may wish to consider include:

• Nazi methods of control and propaganda
• Whether most Germans were as helpless as they claimed
• Were these guards forced to join the SS?
• The example of Germans who did resist.

Present your views to the rest of the class and then try to reach a conclusion. Use the cards below to write brief prompts to help you. This is much more effective than simply reading out your report.

Issue: Control and propaganda

Issue: Were the Germans as helpless as they claimed?

Issue: Were these guards forced to join the SS?

Issue: The example of Germans who did resist

The USA 1919–1941

Key features of the chapter

	Issue(s) covered	Assessment elements	Format(s) for pupil work
Focus Task (p.147): Economic boom	What caused the boom?	Use of sources, selecting and deploying knowledge	Research, presentation in chart
Focus Task (p.152): The boom	What factors caused the boom?	Use of sources, selecting and deploying knowledge	Source based research – extended writing
Focus Task (p.153): Agriculture	Why did agriculture not share in the prosperity?	Key features of historical situation	Research, letter to the President (extended writing)
Focus Task (p.155): The boom	Did all Americans share in the boom?	Use of sources, selecting and deploying knowledge	Source based research – extended writing
Focus Task (p.157): The Roaring Twenties	Features of the Roaring Twenties	Key features of historical situation, selecting and deploying knowledge	Research, summary diagram
Activity (p.159): Immigration	Aspects of immigrant life	Key features of historical situation, use of sources	Research, poster
Activity (p.161): Black people in the USA	Experiences in 1920s USA	Selecting and deploying knowledge, historical personalities	Radio interview, report/handbook
Focus Task (p.162): Attitudes in the 1920s	Intolerance in 1920s USA	Selecting and deploying knowledge, use of sources	Research, chart format, extended writing
Focus Task (p.165): Prohibition	Why was Prohibition introduced and then abolished?	Cause, knowledge	Research, letters to Congress
Focus Task (p.167): Changes in 1920s	How was US changing in 1920s?	Use of sources, change	Overview report
Focus Task (p.169): Wall Street Crash	Was speculation responsible?	Cause, use of sources, selecting and deploying knowledge	Discussion groups, extended writing
Focus Task (p.170): Effects of Crash	Impact of Crash on US economy	Cause, use of sources, selecting and deploying knowledge	Causal diagram, research task
Focus Task (p.172): The Crash	Human impact of the Crash	Cause, use of sources	Selecting photos and commentary
Focus Task (p.174): 1932 election	Why did Roosevelt win?	Cause, selecting and deploying knowledge, historical perspectives	Research, extended writing
Focus Task (p.177): New Deal	What was the New Deal?	Describing and explaining issues	Research, producing summary articles
Focus Task (p.179): New Deal after 1933	Changes in New Deal	Change, selecting and deploying knowledge	Research, table highlighting change
Focus Task (p.181): Opposition to New Deal	Why people opposed the New Deal	Personalities, key features of historical situation	Research, table, extended writing
Focus Task (p.182): Success of the New Deal	How successful was the New Deal?	Key features, change, selecting and deploying knowledge	Research, planning and extended writing

Part 1 WHAT WAS AMERICA LIKE IN THE 1920S?

What was the 'boom'? – the Issue Starter

Pupils are directed straight to the heart of the issue through the array of sources on pages 146–147. These visual sources are deliberately accompanied by explanatory text to put them into context – which is essential if pupils are to use usual visual material effectively. **Questions 1 and 2** could be addressed as written tasks or in small-group discussion. Whatever the methodology, pupils should enjoy and benefit from breaking down the visual sources into the components of information they contain. In this context **question 3**, the definition of the term 'boom', is a crucial exercise.

Why was there an economic boom in the 1920s?

This long and fairly detailed section sets out why the USA experienced such dramatic growth in the 1920s. The emphasis is on narrative text and on statistical data, encouraging pupils to integrate their findings from the two. **Questions 1 and 2** on **page 150** are intermediaries – best tackled orally but introducing pupils to the ways in which the same statistical data can be interpreted differently.

The Focus Task on page 152 demands that pupils have an overview of the section. The metaphor of the skyscraper will not be lost on them, but the information which they add is important. It is also important that parameters such as space/word limit are set, to discourage copying. Pupils could be encouraged to use bullet points of, say, ten words only. This process should equip them well for part 2, which lends itself to extended writing. **Worksheet 6.1** provides a framework for the whole task, including a structure for a written answer for part 2.

Problems in the farming industry

Having examined the spectacular heights of the American economy, pupils now turn to ask 'Was it all so good?'. In this section they examine American agriculture. The section consists of a long and fairly detailed narrative which should provide pupils with more than adequate raw material for the **Focus Task** on **page 153**. For weaker pupils, **Worksheet 6.2** will provide a framework into which they can 'slot' the necessary raw material. As an extension exercise, perhaps for more able pupils, pupils could be asked to formulate Hoover's reply to the letter.

Did all Americans benefit from the boom?

In studying farming, pupils will have encountered the issue of America's poor whites and rural Blacks. Using the text and the array of sources pupils should get a clear impression of the contrasts in American society. The **Focus Task** on **page 155** pulls this together very clearly. For the task, teachers may wish to set parameters such as word limits or demand the inclusion of, for example, at least one visual or statistical source. The essence is that the report presents two contrasting pictures, and that pupils balance the evidence in reaching a conclusion. Although a valuable skill in its own right, this is also a skill pupils will have to apply in examinations. **Worksheet 6.3** provides a framework for the report.

The USA in the Roaring Twenties

This section attempts to introduce pupils to the spirit of the 1920s, something which is easy to identify but rather more difficult to define. The section is broken up into the key features which must have most readily struck observers both within and from outside the USA. At the same time the section also raises the point that many Americans were disturbed by the changes they saw in the 1920s.

Question 1 on page 156 concentrates, however, on the optimistic and carefree spirit of the 1920s. The creation of a slogan is a way into this spirit, since a slogan can be a powerful tool for expressing a mood. **Question 2** is also well suited to an oral approach.

The **Focus Task**, although short, is extremely demanding. Pupils needing a push start could be directed towards a simple cloud-diagram format, using the subheadings in the text as guidelines for the individual clouds. Alternatively, pupils could focus on the source materials, selecting representative sources and explaining their choice. **Worksheet 6.4** details some of these possibilities.

Was immigration policy racist?

This section makes pupils aware of a new twist in the tale of 1920s America. The previous section will have alerted them to some of the underlying tensions in the USA. In this section pupils should appreciate the many and varied backgrounds of Americans but also come to terms with the problems which this issue was beginning to cause by the 1920s. Pupils could profitably devote time to looking carefully at the text in this section before jumping into **questions 1–3** on **page 159**. Pupils could tackle question 1 by 'pairing' the concerns raised in each of the two sources. Question 2 is more of a general discussion question and should provide avenues of discussion which help pupils formulate their ideas on question 3.

The Activity on page 159 builds from these questions, and **Worksheet 6.5** provides a template for the activity. The main aim is for pupils to grasp both the positive and negative sides of the experiences of immigrants in the USA.

The experience of Black people

While the previous section hinted at the darker side of the USA, this section will leave pupils in little doubt. It is perhaps worth taking the time for the whole class to read **page 160** out loud and absorb the power of James Cameron's words. The remainder of the section sets out the mixed, but generally downward, fortunes of Blacks who either remained in the South or migrated to northern towns and cities. The **Activity** on Paul Robeson on **page 161** is best suited to a small-group discussion followed by a 'plenary' session. It is worth pointing out the high profile of Robeson, which is perhaps on a par with that of OJ Simpson in 1996.

The other **Activity** clearly merits a written response. Pupils could use the three subheadings in this section as titles for paragraphs. As on Worksheet 6.4, they might also wish to select seminal sources to support their work.

The Monkey Trial

This section is useful in rounding off the issue of intolerance and the darker aspects of American society in the period. **Questions 1 and 2** should help pupils draw their conclusions on the whole issue as well as focusing on religious fundamentalism. The **Focus Task** on **page 162** provides the framework for pupils to pull together their work on intolerance. **Worksheet 6.6** provides further support for pupils and extension work.

Prohibition – did the Americans make a mistake?

This is perhaps the best-known and most evocative of all of the issues associated with the USA in the 1920s. **Sources 42 and 43**, and the questions associated with them, take pupils straight to the heart of why prohibition was introduced. **Questions 1–3** on **page 164** are suited to discussion, although 2 and 3 might also elicit useful written answers from pupils. Similarly, the main aim of **question 4** on **page 165** is to keep pupils focused, and to stimulate their thinking for the **Focus Task** on **page 165**.

The essence of the Focus Task is for pupils to understand the motives of the 'noble experiment' but also to see that *with hindsight* Americans recognised that prohibition had failed. **Worksheet 6.7** provides a structure for their letters.

Women in 1920s America

This section looks at another important aspect of the USA, and takes pupils towards the conclusion of this part of the chapter. **Questions 1 and 2** on **page 166** exercise pupils' ability to interpret visual sources but also to go a step further from this analysis. The differences between the two sources should not prove difficult to spot, but identifying the contextual factors responsible for the change requires a sophisticated level of understanding.

Question 3 on page 167 directs pupils toward the contrasting view of the position of women in the 1920s. These three questions, when taken together, provide a framework for writing at length on this issue. **Worksheet 6.8** suggests a framework for this, since many pupils may wish to go into the topic in some depth. The question should raise three key issues:

- How women did gain greater freedom
- Ways in which life remained much the same
- The extent of freedom gained.

The Focus Task on page 167 asks pupils to renew all of their work in this part of the chapter before looking at the next, and very different, period in American history.

Part 2 THE WALL STREET CRASH

What caused the Wall Street Crash?

The 1920s close with this most spectacular and far-reaching event. Teachers may wish to direct pupils first to the **Factfile** on **page 169** and ask them to look carefully at the **Focus Task**. This should give them an overview of events and familiarity with their 'brief' before they read the chapter. **Worksheet 6.9** should help pupils to organise their thoughts on this issue and provide training for the next Focus Task.

The consequences of the Wall Street Crash

The impact of the Crash on the American economy is fundamental to the remaining sections of the chapter. Pupils could use the principles employed in the previous Focus Task to structure their work in the **Focus Task** on **page 170**. The respective importance of the various factors is less relevant, and it may be that a flow-chart format is more appropriate than a cloud diagram. The key issue is that of interconnected events. As with the previous Focus Task, the lines which connect events need to be explained and substantiated. Every pupil should be able to 'justify the lines'. The follow-up research task is an opportunity for pupils to use a wider range of resources. For specific research such as this, the CD-ROM is a particularly valuable tool.

The human cost of the Depression

In this section the emphasis is on pupils examining a range of evidence and drawing conclusions for themselves. As always, to make sense sources must be placed in context. Thus the **Focus Task** on **page 172** concentrates on one type of evidence – photographs – and asks pupils to show an understanding of how a photograph, given its context, can be illustrative of a period, movement or events. **Worksheet 6.10** supports the task.

The 1932 presidential election

This section aims to provide a powerful narrative which will give pupils a feel for the charisma of Roosevelt and the powerful momentum which he had built up even before he officially took office as President. **Questions 3 and 1** on **pages 173 and 174** are important in this respect and should be tackled as written exercises. Pupils' answers will provide the raw material for the **Focus Task** on **page 174**. The **Activity** immediately before the Focus Task is an ideal vehicle for class or small-group discussion. The Focus Task is straightforward in that it demands a written, mainly narrative account. Abler pupils might be more challenged by changing the emphasis of the question to, for example, 'Did Roosevelt win the 1932 election or did Hoover lose it?'.

Part 3   FRANKLIN D ROOSEVELT AND THE NEW DEAL

The Hundred Days

The aim of this section is to capture the determination and energy of the Hundred Days and the first New Deal. The questions on **pages 175–176** provide ideal bases for discussion which will allow pupils to get their teeth into the issues. Similarly the range of visual sources should allow pupils of all abilities to appreciate the aims of the New Deal and the TVA. The **Focus Task** on **page 177** draws on all of this material and asks pupils to make the sources really work in a context. **Worksheet 6.11** provides guidance.

The Second New Deal

The Focus Task in the previous section will have raised in pupils' minds some of the problems associated with carrying out a programme as ambitious as the New Deal. **Questions 1–3** on **page 179** are ideally suited to discussion, but do target important skills of source evaluation. They elicit useful information and ideas for the **Focus Task** on **page 179** but also provide some food for thought for the next section. **Worksheet 6.12** provides a framework for the Focus Task.

Opposition to the New Deal, 1936

In contrast to some of the earlier sections, this topic is dealt with mainly through an extended narrative. However, **questions 1 and 2** on **page 180**, dealing with relatively light-hearted sources, should help pupils to get a feel for the key issues. The **Focus Task** on **page 181** is supported by **Worksheet 6.13**.

Was the New Deal a success?

The final section pulls together this part of the chapter. The issues are clearly set out in bullet points. A useful strategy might be for pupils to work in groups, thrashing out their responses to **questions 3–5** on **page 181**. Having done this, they should be well equipped to tackle the highly structured **Focus Task** at the end of the chapter.

What factors caused the economic boom?

1 Look back over pages 148–152 and complete the diagram below. Remember to keep your points brief or you will run out of space. Also remember that you are looking for causes.

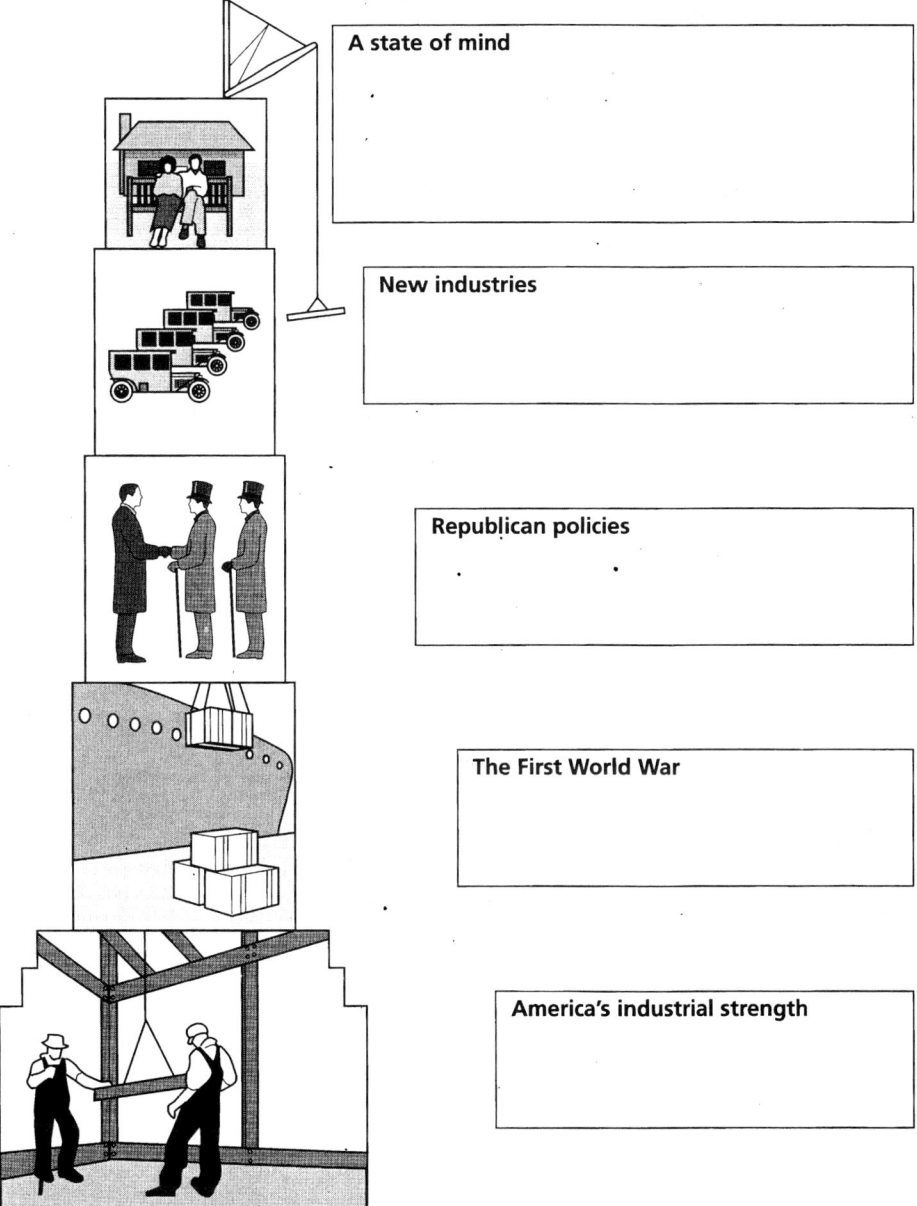

A state of mind

New industries

Republican policies

The First World War

America's industrial strength

2 One historian has said, 'Without the new automobile industry the prosperity of the 1920s would scarcely have been possible'.

Explain whether you agree or disagree with this statement. You should organise your answer into paragraphs.
Paragraph 1: Introduction – what the question is about.
Paragraph 2: Why the automobile industry was so important (use lots of examples).
Paragraph 3: Other industries which were important.
Paragraph 4: Other factors (e.g. politics, events outside USA) which were important.
Paragraph 5: Your conclusion (yes, no, hard to say).

Why did agriculture not prosper in the USA in the 1920s?

AIM

To investigate and explain the reasons why American farmers struggled in the 1920s

RESOURCES

Farmers became the fiercest critics of the policies of the Republican Party. Write a letter from a farmer to the Republican President, Calvin Coolidge, to complain about Republican policies. Explain to the President why farming is in such a poor state and why it matters that his government do something about it.

You may find the ideas below helpful.

Dear Mr President

Allow me to introduce myself. I am ………… from …………. Until about 1919 I owned a fairly prosperous small farm, but now I am facing ruin.

We are facing many problems, Mr President. For example:

* _____

* _____

* _____

I admit, we have caused some of the problems ourselves by:

* _____

* _____

* _____

But other problems are beyond our control. They were caused by:

* _____

* _____

* _____

Mr President, we farmers are a large part of American society and the situation is serious. You must do something about it because if it continues . . .

* _____

* _____

* _____

Please help us.

Yours

Did all Americans share in the boom?

AIM

To identify and explain inequalities in US society

RESOURCES

In 1928, a new Republican President, Herbert Hoover, took office. He said *'One of the oldest and perhaps noblest human activities (aims) has been the abolition of poverty ... we in America today are nearer to the final triumph over poverty than ever before in the history of any land'.*

1 Working in pairs, investigate Hoover's claim. One of you look for evidence which supports Hoover's view, the other for opposing evidence. Note down your findings.

Source (authorship, origin or section of text)	How it supports or opposes Hoover's claim	Quality of this evidence (your view)

2 Now work together to produce an advisory report for the new President. As you plan your report you must think about:

- the key points you are trying to make
- whether your report presents a fully balanced picture of all aspects of the USA
- what evidence you will use to convince the President that you are right.

You may wish to use this structure for your report.
Paragraph 1: How the USA appears to outsiders
Paragraph 2: America's successes in the 1920s and which groups in society are enjoying them
Paragraph 3: Any economic problems you find and which groups are suffering from them
Paragraph 4: Your conclusion.

WORSHEET *The Roaring Twenties*

6.4

AIM

To use a range of sources to describe the spirit and key aspects of 1920s USA

RESOURCES

1 Fill in this diagram to summarise the features of The Roaring Twenties. Use the text on pages 156 and 157 but add other features you are aware of from earlier in this chapter or from your wider reading.

Entertainment:

- _____
- _____
- _____
- _____
- _____
- _____
- _____

Cities:

- _____
- _____
- _____
- _____
- _____
- _____
- _____

The car:

- _____
- _____
- _____
- _____
- _____
- _____
- _____

Morals:

- _____
- _____
- _____
- _____
- _____
- _____
- _____

2 Look at pages 156 and 157.
   a) Choose four sources, at least two of them written (these could be extracts from the text), which you believe represent the spirit of the 1920s.
   b) For each source, explain why you have chosen it.
   c) Now explain how the four sources together represent the Roaring Twenties.

WORKSHEET

6.5

Immigrants at Ellis Island

AIM

To use evidence and examples to identify and explain the different experiences of immigrants

RESOURCES

Using the outlines below sketch or plan out your poster to be displayed in the immigrant reception area on Ellis Island, New York. You should either:

a) warn immigrants of the problems they might face in the USA; or

b) encourage them to see the opportunities that America offers to immigrants.

**WHAT TO EXPECT
IN AMERICA**

**AMERICA: THE LAND
OF OPPORTUNITY!**

Before you begin your sketch or plan, you must research the issues and decide what messages you wish your posters to send. If you include more than four or five key points your poster will look overcrowded. Use the points below as a checklist:

- Four or five points decided?
- These to be put across by image, words or both?
- How will I grab people's attention (e.g. Sacco and Vanzetti case)?
- What background images will I use?

WORSHEET

6.6

How widespread was intolerance in the USA in the 1920s?

AIM

To describe and explain the extent of intolerance in 1920s USA

RESOURCES

Look back at your work on immigrants, Black people and other aspects of the 1920s and complete the chart below.

Group	How did prejudice or intolerance affect them (give examples)?	How did they react?

EXTENSION WORK

Use your findings to write an answer of about 200 words to this question: 'America in the 1920s was fine, but only if you were white'. Do you feel that this is an accurate summary of the period or is it over-simplified?

You will need to organise your answer into paragraphs.
1 Your views on the question
2 Whether all white people were happy
3 The fate of Black people
4 How the statement could be improved (e.g. by referring to other minorities).

Why was prohibition introduced in 1919 and then abolished in 1933?

AIM

To use a range of sources and other evidence to explain changing attitudes to prohibition

RESOURCES

Many people who were convinced of the case for prohibition in 1919 were equally convinced it should be abolished in 1933.

Write two letters.

The first should be from a supporter of prohibition to their Congressman in 1919 explaining why they want their Congressman to vote for prohibition. In your letter explain how prohibition could help solve problems in America.

The second letter should be from the same person to their Congressman in 1933 explaining why they want their Congressman to vote against prohibition. In your letter explain why prohibition has failed.

Your letters might look like this:

1919
Dear Congressman
I write to encourage you to vote for prohibition and to explain
my reasons. Firstly, many respectable people support
prohibition (give plenty of examples)
Secondly, American workers would benefit (explain how this
would happen)
Also, families would be happier if alcohol were banned
(explain this)
There is also the fact that both here and abroad alcohol causes
unpleasant behaviour (give examples)
Yours

1933
Dear Congressman
I last wrote to you about prohibition in 1919. At that time I
supported it but no longer.
To begin with enforcement seems impossible (examples)
Prohibition has also had a corrupting influence (examples)
Gangsters seem to have profited from it (examples)
I feel that the experiment has failed.
Yours

6.8

Women in 1920s America

'The 1920s brought a revolution in freedom and opportunity for women.' Explain whether you agree with this statement.

The main issue in this question is:

_____

_____

_____

_____

_____

_____

The 1920s certainly did bring new freedom and opportunities to women:

_____

_____

_____

_____

_____

_____

On the other hand, for many women, life remained the same:

_____

_____

_____

_____

_____

_____

On balance, the evidence seem to suggest that for most women . . .

_____

_____

_____

_____

_____

_____

WORKSHEET

How far was speculation responsible for the Wall Street Crash?

AIM

To analyse and explain the relative importance of different causes of the Wall Street Crash

RESOURCES

Look at the diagram below which shows some of the factors which led to the Wall Street Crash.

1 Add a brief note alongside each one to explain how it helped cause the Crash.
2 Add other factors to the diagram if you think they are important.

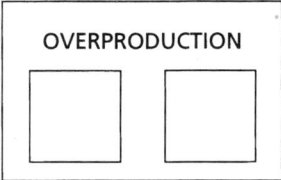

OVERPRODUCTION

WALL STREET CRASH

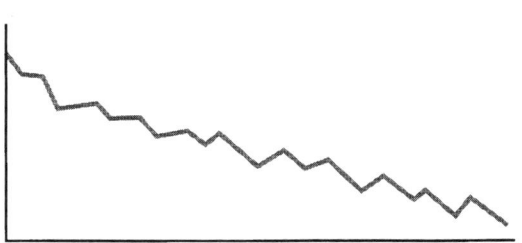

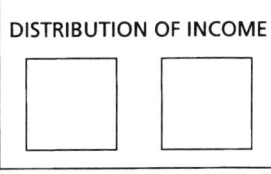

DISTRIBUTION OF INCOME

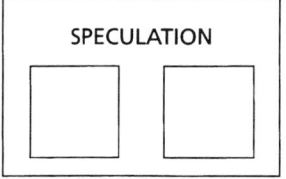

SPECULATION

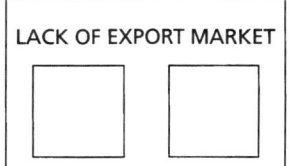

ACTION OF BANKS

LACK OF EXPORT MARKET

3 In one of the smaller boxes under each factor, put a letter to show what kind of cause it was:
   S short-term; **M** medium-term; **L** long-term.
4 In the other box, give the factor a mark out of 10 for its importance. Discuss this mark with a partner.
5 Draw lines to join the factors to show which ones you believe are connected. Use a key or write on each line an explanation of why you have drawn it.

EXTENSION WORK

Choose the three most important causes of the Wall Street Crash. These will be the ones you gave the highest score to.

Write an essay to explain whether one of these is more important than the others.
Organise your answer in paragraphs:

Paragraph 1: What the question is about
Paragraph 2: How and why 1 was a factor
Paragraph 3: How and why 2 was a factor and whether it was linked to 1
Paragraph 4: How and why 3 was a factor and whether it was linked to 1 and 2
Paragraph 5: Your conclusion (e.g. 1, 2 or 3 is more important; they are all equal in importance; impossible to say because they were all linked).

WORKSHEET
6.10 The human consequences of the Depression

AIM

To use a range of evidence to describe and explain the impact of the Depression

RESOURCES

You have been asked to prepare an exhibition of photographs which compares the life of Americans during the boom times of the 1920s with the depressed years of the 1930s. Look at Chapter 6 and choose two pictures from the 1920s and two from the 1930s which you think present the greatest contrast.

(i) Explain (a) why you have chosen those particular pictures and (b) the contrasts they show.

(ii) For the 1920s and 1930s select one written source which seems to go well with your photos and explain your choice.

1920s   Photo 1 (Source. . . . .)   Photo 2 (Source. . . . .)

Description of photo:	Description of photo:
caption _____	caption _____

1930s   Photo 1 (Source. . . . .)   Photo 2 (Source. . . . .)

Description of photo:	Description of photo:
caption _____	caption _____

EXTENSION WORK

'The Depression hit all Americans equally hard.' Does the evidence support this view?

STEP 1
Examine Sources 6–11 on pages 171–172 and complete the table below.

Source	Supports the view?	Is it convincing evidence?
Source 6 Source 7 Source 8 Source 9 Source 10 Source 11 Text		

STEP 2
Now answer the question in paragraphs.

1) The evidence does/does not support the view (your opinion).

2) Sources 00–00 show that ...
Their evidence is convincing because ...
On the other hand we must be aware that ...

3) Sources 00–00 seem to suggest a different story ...
However, this is less convincing because ...

4) In conclusion ...

What was the New Deal of 1933?

AIM

To define the key features of the New Deal and describe attitudes to it

RESOURCES

Work in pairs. One of you is working for a pro-New Deal newspaper, the other for an anti-New Deal newspaper. It is 16 June 1933. You have each been asked to write an account of what measures the Roosevelt administration has introduced in its first hundred days.

These items will need to appear in both of your articles:

• A description of the measures introduced by Roosevelt
• A description of the reasons these measures were introduced.

Your articles will differ over

• whether the measures will work
• whether the cost is worth paying.

Use the advice below to get ideas on how to write your article. It is possible that some evidence can be used in both articles.

The anti-New Deal article

Think about how your article might criticise these measures. Remember that:

a) Roosevelt's opponents were against the government spending more money.
b) They thought the Depression was not America's fault and that economic problems could not be solved by government action.
c) They thought that helping people who were suffering because of the Depression would make them lazy and unable to help themselves.
d) In their opinion Roosevelt hadn't thought out his ideas very carefully.

How can you work these viewpoints into your article and headline? The following words might help you: spendthrift, interfering, un-American, misguided, badly thought out.

The pro-New Deal article

Think about how your article might praise these measures. Remember that:

a) Roosevelt's supporters felt that a decisive government was needed who showed they were prepared to take action.
b) They felt that all other attempts to solve the problems of the Depression had failed.
c) They believed that the main aim was to get people back to work and to increase people's confidence.

How can you work these viewpoints into your article and headline? The following words might help you: dynamic, creative, decisive, caring, new, confidence.

Begin your article like this:

YOUR HEADLINE: _____

In just one hundred days President Roosevelt has revealed exactly what he means by his New Deal! He has...

WORSHEET

6.12

How did the character of the New Deal change after 1933?

AIM

To identify and explain differences in the New Deal after 1933

RESOURCES

1 Use the chart below to list the main characteristics of the New Deal in 1933 and after.

Characteristics of the New Deal, 1933	Characteristics of the Second New Deal

3 Use the chart and the evidence of pages 177–179 to decide which of these two statements seems to be the most reasonable explanation of differences between the First and Second New Deals.

Explanation 1: Roosevelt made many mistakes in 1933 and his critics forced him to alter the New Deal.

Explanation 2: Roosevelt used the Second New Deal to build on the achievements of the Hundred Days.

For each explanation say
(i) What evidence seems to support it
(ii) Whether you agree with it – wholly, partly or not at all.

Take care to explain your answers fully.

WORKSHEET

6.13

Why did some people oppose the New Deal?

AIM

To use a range of sources to describe and explain the motives of critics of the New Deal

RESOURCES

1 Look back over pages 179–181 and complete the table.

Group	Reasons for opposing New Deal	How far was their opposition a danger to the New Deal?

2 Write a report of about 150–200 words answering the critics of the New Deal on behalf of President Roosevelt. As you deal with each of the groups you should cover:

- their *real* motives for opposing the New Deal (if you think their true motives were different from what they actually said)
- what achievements or other points you believe answer their criticisms.

SECTION 3: CO-OPERATION AND CONFLICT 1919–1945

The League of Nations

Key features of the chapter

	Issue(s) covered	Assessment elements	Format(s) for pupil work
Focus Task (p.187): USA and League	Why did the USA not join the League?	Cause, selecting and deploying knowledge	Written report
Activity (p.187): Views on League	Contemporary views on League of Nations	Use of sources	Analysis of cartoons
Activity (p.191): League organisation	League bodies and agencies	Historical knowledge	Guide book entry
Focus Task (p.191): League structure	Were there weaknesses in the organisation?	Selecting and deploying knowledge, interpretations	Hypothetical discussion
Focus Task (p.192): League in action	Was the League successful in solving disputes in the 1920s?	Selecting and deploying knowledge, key features of historical situations	Rating League's performance in 1920s
Focus Task (p.194): League in action	Was the League unable to act?	Selecting and deploying, use of sources, interpretations	Testing hypotheses against evidence
Focus Task (p.198): League in the 1920s	How successful was the League in the 1920s?	Interpretations, use of sources, describing and explaining events	Examining record of League against objectives
Activity (p. 205): Abyssinian crisis	The escalation of the crisis	Historical knowledge, role of personalities	Timeline of crisis
Focus Task (p. 209): Failure of the League	Why did the League fail?	Cause, historical knowledge	Analysing causes of failure

Part 1 HOW SUCCESSFUL WAS THE LEAGUE IN THE 1920S?

The birth of the League – the Issue Starter

Material for an issue starter for this chapter can be located in Chapters 1 and 2. Chapter 1 highlights the secrecy and jealous rivalry which made possible the outbreak of World War I. Chapter 2 contains a wealth of evidence as to why the motivation of the founders of the League, particularly Wilson, was 'Never again!'.

Question 1 on page 185 raises this question as a basis for discussion. The myriad possibilities and complications of this question make it best suited to a teacher-led discussion. Teachers may wish to throw in these extra questions:

• What might go wrong with each of the three types of suggested League?
• How could these problems be prepared for?

A body blow to the League

There are a number of issues which pupils must address in this section. That the absence of the USA was a blow can bc taken as read. The crucial points from the section are:

• Why did the USA refuse to join?
• What were the implications of this for the League?

Question 2 on page 185 brings pupils immediately into the issue of the USA's refusal to join. Pupils will need to look carefully at the points raised in Source 4 before summarising them in the slogan. The **Activity** on **page 187** asks pupils to put two sources into a context and analyse the message of each accordingly. **Worksheet 7.1** should help pupils to pursue this activity in a structured manner.

The **Focus Task** on **page 187** could be used as an opportunity to respond to the criticism implicit in the cartoons. Some pupils may need a few hints and prompts in order to put together their report. These can be found on **Worksheet 7.2**.

How did the League of Nations work?

Leadership of the League

This section is short but pivotal, in that it sets out the responsibilities which fell on to the shoulders of Britain and France. The section also sets out the extent to which these two powers were unready for the responsibility and also not entirely willing to take it on. **Questions 2–4** on **page 189** could be tackled as discussion or as written exercises. Whatever the format, pupils will need to carry them out as preparation for the **Focus Task** on **page 191**.

The structure of the League of Nations

The central focus of this section is clearly on **Source 12** which is packed with information. Both the Activity and the Focus Task are aimed at helping pupils to decode and make manageable the information load.

The **Activity** uses **Source 11** as an intermediary device. Pupils can show their understanding at a range of levels. In the first instance they must clearly link the activities in the murals with the relevant agencies. Secondly, the guide-book entry task could be made more or less challenging by adapting the parameters of the task:

• The length of entries
• Depth of detail about the work
• Examples of the agencies' work (later in the chapter)
• The use of or location of seminal sources.

Pupils might also leave a space and add a post-1939 postscript on each of the entries later on.

The **Focus Task** is rather broader in its aim and scope. The key aim is that pupils recognise the mixed views about the League in 1920. There was great optimism but there were also reservations. The medium chosen, that of the two hypothetical diplomats, is designed to make these somewhat arcane concepts more human. The two diplomats also crop up again as a perspective device later in the chapter (question 3, page 194). Some pupils will find the support in **Worksheet 7.3** helpful.

Was the League good at settling border disputes in the 1920s?

This section is quite long and requires pupils to hold a good deal of information and ideas in their heads for a period of time. For this reason the **Focus Task** on **page 192** comes early in the section. It should help pupils to focus on the task and give purpose to their reading. By using the table format on **Worksheet 7.4** they can make the events and issues of the period visible at a glance.

The narrative which follows **Source 14** integrates sources and text and questions 1–3 on **page 193**, the sources being given greater value by their context. **Questions 1 and 2** require pupils to comprehend the sources but also to think laterally by referencing their answers from the accompanying text. **Question 3** is suitable for discussion or written answers and it carries the potential to be greatly extended. However, as it stands it is aimed at preparing pupils for the Focus Task at the end of the section. This also applies to **questions 5 and 6**, which return to the process of putting sources into a context. Having worked through the questions, pupils should be in a strong position to pull together their work in the table format used in the **Focus Task** on **page 194**. **Worksheet 7.5** provides a pro forma for this. It is important to remind pupils of the need to keep their work safe but accessible, as they will be using it later in the chapter.

How did the League of Nations work for a better world?

The focus of this section tends to be overlooked because the history of the period is dominated by great events on the political scene. However, the work of the League's agencies probably reached more people than its attempts to bestride the world's political problems. **Questions 4–6** on **page 195** allow for an oral or written approach, and the topic is well suited to further investigation in project and enquiry work.

What did the League do about disarmament in the 1920s?

The relatively upbeat narrative on the work of the League now begins to change, as the emphasis shifts to the issues on which the League struggled to make progress. **Questions 1–2** on **page 196** indirectly stress the importance of viewing sources and evidence in context. The questions hinge on **Source 21**, which warns of making excessively harsh judgements with the benefit of hindsight. Pupils need to be aware of the real euphoria and relief which accompanied the announcement of the Locarno Treaties.

The remainder of the section deals with the other international agreements which were drawn up in the 1920s. Pupils need to be familiar with the aims and terms of the agreements. They also need to consider the impact of these treaties on the credibility of the League. **Questions 2–5** on **page 198** take pupils into these issues and could be dealt with through discussion or as a written exercise. An alternative approach is presented on **Worksheet 7.6**.

The final **Focus Task** of this section is a structured review of the record of the League in the 1920s. Pupils must look back over their work and reach substantiated judgements on the successes and failures of the League. **Worksheet 7.5** provides extra support for this process.

Part 2 WHY DID THE LEAGUE FAIL IN THE 1930S?

How did the economic depression harm the work of the League?

This is the first of several sections whose main purpose is to recount the declining fortunes of the League. Pupils should be informed of this, and teachers may find it profitable to introduce pupils to the final Focus Task on page 209. Having looked at the task, pupils can then read and answer the questions with the task in mind.

Worksheet 7.7, which could be enlarged to A3, may be useful as a guide for keeping track of events as pupils work through the next sections. For this section, pupils must emphasise the secondary importance or 'knock-on' effect of the Depression.

Why did the Japanese invade Manchuria?

Along with Abyssinia this event is, of course, a crucial test case for the League. The Japanese situation is clearly set out and pupils will have to think hard in order to reduce the necessary points down to a form which will fit on **Worksheet 7.7**. The section includes three important questions, which probably merit written answers, although pupils could profitably spend much time discussing them. **Question 1,** *Why did disarmament fail?* on **page 204** certainly requires a written response, although disarmament is covered in **Worksheet 7.7**.

How did Mussolini's invasion of Abyssinia damage the League?

This section charts the crisis which effectively destroyed the League. Pupils can use the timeline format suggested in the **Activity** on **page 205** to keep track of a sometimes bewildering sequence of events. **Questions 1–3** on **page 207** are rather more reflective and ask pupils again to see the context of a number of sources. They should then complete the timeline and **Worksheet 7.7**.

A disaster for the League and for the world

The purpose of this section is to reflect on the disastrous consequences for the League of the Abyssinian crisis and to set pupils up for the concluding **Focus Task (page 209)**. This task is supported by **Worksheet 7.8.**

The original captions for the *Punch* cartoons in Source 23 were as follows: **A** 'I'm afraid her constitution isn't all it should be, but we mustn't give up hope yet.' **B** 'I had hoped for a better job than this.'

WORSHEET

7.1

The USA refuses to join the League – views from the time

AIM

To analyse primary sources on the USA's refusal to join the League

RESOURCES

Work in pairs. One of you work with Source 1A and the other with Source 1B.

Use the following guidelines to analyse the cartoons:

Background
- The date it was drawn – what else was going on at the same time?
- The country and the type of publication where the cartoon was published (e.g. a British newspaper which supported a harsh treaty).

Words
- Look at the caption (if the cartoon has one) – it is usually very blunt.
- Many cartoons use labels on the characters or include objects. Look very carefully for these as they give very strong clues as to what the cartoon is about.

The cartoon itself
- Start by looking at the background if there is one. What kind of impression is it trying to give?
- Look at any figures and think about how the cartoonist has drawn them in terms of size, bulk and their position in relation to each other.
- Facial expressions are usually very important – they tell you whether the cartoonist thinks that a character is brave, cowardly, sincere, treacherous etc.

Once you have looked at the cartoons:
1 Decide whether your cartoon is optimistic or pessimistic about the League of Nations.
2 Decide whether your cartoon is critical of the USA.
3 Compare your findings with those of your partner and then write a paragraph (about 75 words) to explain what the message of each cartoon is.

SOURCE 1A

THE GAP IN THE BRIDGE.

SOURCE 1B

READY TO START.

Two British cartoons from 1919/1920. The figure in the white hat represents the USA.

WORKSHEET

7.2

Why did the USA not join the League of Nations?

AIM

To list and explain the reasons why the USA did not join the League

RESOURCES

1 Read over pages 186 and 187 and fill in the diagram below. In the empty boxes fill in reasons why the USA would not join the League. There is space for more clouds if you want to add them.

2 You are the American correspondent of the *Daily Express*. Write a short report for your newspaper, in 1921, explaining why America has not joined the League. Your report should mention:

- factors inside the USA which influenced the decision
- factors outside the USA
- whether you believe Source 6A on page 187 is fair
- what was the main factor, in the end, behind the US decision.

WORSHEET **Were there weaknesses in the League's organisation?**

7.3

AIM

To analyse different views of the structure of the League

RESOURCES

Look at the two views expressed in the cartoon below.

Membership of the League

_____
_____
_____
_____
_____

What the main bodies within the League can do

_____
_____
_____
_____
_____

How each body will make decisions

_____
_____
_____
_____
_____

Enforcing decisions

_____
_____
_____
_____
_____
_____

Work in pairs. Choose one statement each and explain, under the headings provided, why each diplomat feels the way he does. For example, the diplomat on the left feels confident about the League. Why does the League's membership make him feel that way?

The League in action – disputes in the 1920s

AIM

To analyse and evaluate the performance of the League in settling border disputes in the 1920s

RESOURCES

Five of the problems shown in Source 14 are described in the text starting on page 193. As you read about each one score the League's success on the following scale and fill in the table.

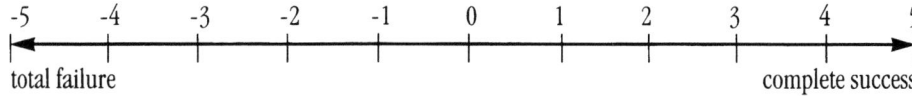

-5   -4   -3   -2   -1   0   1   2   3   4   5

total failure   complete success

Dispute/incident	Score for League	Reason

How successful was the League in the 1920s?

AIM

To reach a supported conclusion on the League's record in the 1920s

RESOURCES

Here are the four main aims of the League:

- To discourage aggression
- To encourage trade and other co-operation
- To encourage disarmament
- To improve living and working conditions of people all over the world.

1 a) For each of these aims explain how far you think the League succeeded in achieving it. Use at least two examples to support your point of view.
   b) Put the objectives in order; most achieved at the top, least at the bottom.

2 For each objective suggest one change the League could make in order to be more effective.

3 Which of these statements do you most agree with?

   (i) The League of Nations was a great force for peace in the 1920s.
   (ii) Events of the 1920s showed just how weak the League really was.
   (iii) The League's successes in the 1920s were small-scale, its failures were more high-profile.

You need to answer this question in paragraphs.

Paragraph 1: Your view of Statement (i) with an explanation of why you accept/reject it . . .

- _____
- _____

Paragraph 2: Your view of Statement (ii) with an explanation of why you accept/reject it . . .

- _____
- _____

Paragraph 3: Your view of Statement (iii) with an explanation of why you accept/reject it . . .

- _____
- _____

Paragraph 4: Your overall view. . .

- _____
- _____

The international agreements of the 1920s

1 Look at the text and sources on pages 196–198 and complete the table below. You will find the Factfile particularly useful.

2 'The international agreements of the 1920s greatly strengthened the position of the League of Nations.' How far do you agree with this statement?

Explain your answer by referring to the work of the League and your table below. Use the headings of each of the columns in the table as headings for paragraphs in your answer.

	Washington Treaty	Rapallo	Dawes Plan	Locarno	Kellogg-Briand	Young Plan
Date						
Aim						
Countries involved						
Terms (how it was meant to work)						
Whether the League was involved						
How it helped/ hindered/did not affect the League's work						

WORKSHEET

7.7

The failure of the League in the 1930s

AIM

To record the key events of the 1930s and the ways in which they affected the League

RESOURCES

As you read through pages 199–207, use the space below to record important points and ideas. Fill in the important details on the 'profiles' of the four main events, but remember you are aiming for a summary, so be brief.

DEPRESSION

Summary _____

_____

Main cause(s) _____

_____

Action by League _____

_____

Effects of event _____
on League

_____

MANCHURIA

Summary _____

_____

Main cause(s) _____

_____

Action by League _____

_____

Effects of event _____
on League

ABYSSINIA

Summary _____

_____

Main cause(s) _____

_____

Action by League _____

_____

Effects of event _____
on League

FAILURE OF THE LEAGUE

DISARMAMENT

Summary _____

_____

Main cause(s) _____

_____

Action by League _____

_____

Effects of event _____
on League

When the boxes are complete, draw lines between events which are connected. Along the lines, briefly explain why you feel there is a connection. Your teacher will ask you to justify any lines that you draw!

WORKSHEET

7.8

Why did the League of Nations fail in the 1930s?

AIM

To evaluate and reach conclusions on the relative importance of different reasons for the failure of the League

RESOURCES

The diagram below is a summary of the main reasons for the failure of the League.

Why did the League of Nations fail?

The self-interest of leading members
The League depended on Britain and France to provide firm support in times of crisis. When conflicts occurred, however, neither the British nor French governments were prepared to abandon their own self-interest to support the League.

America and other important countries were absent
At any one time important countries were not members. Germany was not a member until 1926 and left in 1933. The USSR did not join until 1934 whilst Japan left in 1933 and Italy left in 1937. Most important, the USA was never a member. Without such major powers the League lacked authority and sanctions were not effective.

Economic sanctions did not work
Economic sanctions were supposed to be the League's main weapon, but members of the League did not willingly impose them because they worried that without America they would not work. When they did impose them they were easily broken. The League therefore lacked the muscle to enforce the decisions of its assembly and council.

Lack of troops
If economic sanctions failed, military force was the next option. Yet the League had no armed forces of its own and relied upon the co-operation of its members. Britain and France, however, were not willing to commit troops. At no time did troops ever fight on behalf of the League.

The Treaties it had to uphold were seen as unfair
The League was bound to uphold the peace treaties which had created it. In time, however, it became apparent that some of the terms of those peace treaties were harsh and unjust and needed amending.
This further undermined the League.

Decisions were slow
When a crisis occurred, the League was supposed to act quickly and with determination. In many cases, however, the League met too infrequently and took too long to make decisions. The need for all members to agree on a course of action undermined the strength of the League.

1 The diagram highlights a number of weaknesses in the League.

  a) Explain which weaknesses, in your opinion, played an important part in

  • the Manchurian crisis
  • the failure of disarmament
  • the Abyssinian crisis.

  b) In each case, make sure you include evidence to support what you say.

132

2 'The League failed in the 1930s simply because it faced greater challenges than it faced in the 1920s.' Do you agree?

Use this framework for your answer:

In **paragraph 1** explain whether you agree that the challenges of the 1930s were greater than those of the 1920s. Give your reasons for agreeing or disagreeing.

_____
_____
_____
_____

In **paragraph 2** choose one League success from the 1920s and explain why the League succeeded.

_____
_____
_____
_____

In **paragraph 3** choose one League failure in the 1930s and explain why the League failed.

_____
_____
_____
_____

In **paragraph 4** explain whether the League failed because it faced a bigger challenge, or whether there were other reasons. However, the League could still have succeeded in the 1930s if...

_____
_____
_____
_____

Finally, write your conclusion explaining whether you agree/disagree with the statement and why.

_____
_____
_____
_____

Causes of the Second World War

Key features of the chapter

	Issue covered	Assessment elements	Format(s) for pupil work
Activity (p.211): Hitler's plans	Analysing Hitler's ambitions	Analysing sources and key features of historical situation	Briefing paper for British government
Focus Task (p.212): Treaty of Versailles	Hitler's responses to Treaty of Versailles	Analysing events	Recording table
Focus Task (p.217): The 1930s	Consequences of the League's failure	Use of sources, selecting and deploying knowledge	Listing key points and extended writing
Activity (p.222): Munich Agreement	Different perspectives on Munich	Selecting and deploying knowledge, using sources, analysing events	Contrasting newspaper headlines
Focus Task (p.226): Appeasement	Was Appeasement justified?	Selecting and deploying knowledge, using sources, analysing events	Table and extended writing
Focus Task (p.226): Outbreak of war	The cause of the war	Analysing events	Extended writing
Focus Task (p.231): Extension of war	Why did the USA enter the war?	Use of sources, analysing events	Speech for Roosevelt

Part 1 WHY DID PEACE COLLAPSE IN EUROPE IN 1939?

Hitler's plans – the Issue Starter

The issue starter here is contained within the opening section. The seminal question, upon which pupils must develop a reasoned and substantiated opinion, is perhaps that of Hitler's motives. As the first step towards tackling this, they should assess the international ramifications of the Treaty of Versailles. The **Focus Task** on **page 212** should help pupils here, as they will need to hold a good deal of information in their short-term memory. **Worksheet 8.1** provides a format for this task. As well as making a difficult concept visual, the table should be able to double up as a timeline. Finally, the process of moving through the chapter and then coming back to review events will help pupils with revision.

Question 1 on page 211 continues this process of evaluation and review, although teachers might wish to discuss the question with pupils with the help of a map. Clearly, Hitler's personality and the validity of *Mein Kampf* as an accurate indicator of his intentions must be considered.

The Activity on page 211 should help pupils to collate their thoughts on Hitler's plans and at the same time appreciate the difficult position in which the British government found itself. **Worksheet 8.2** provides a framework to help pupils structure their report. With a little adaptation, the report could become a 'third person' activity, based on a question such as 'Why was Britain unsure about Hitler in 1933?'.

Hitler's actions

Hitler's actions are then presented in the form of a narrative, linked closely to a number of key sources. The timeline should help pupils establish an overview of the forthcoming events. At the same time, the question of Hitler the gambler versus Hitler the schemer should be raised in pupils' minds. **Questions 1–3** on **page 213** are predominantly intermediary questions, keeping pupils in tune with events and their implications. Question 1 focuses on the justifications which Hitler used for rearmament. It is important to recognise that, even after World War I, large-scale armament programmes were to some extent regarded as a 'right'. They were not necessarily indicators of aggressive intentions, up to 1936 at least. Also, the view of rearmament as a weapon against unemployment was hard to refute.

Much is made of the Rhineland in this section, because it always raises the question of what might have been, if Hitler had been resisted. The text stresses the extreme risk Hitler was taking. However, **questions 1–3** on **pages 214 and 215** try to establish in pupils' minds that matters were not so clear cut in 1936. Questions 1 and 2 direct pupils to the fears of German strength as reflected in **Source 11**. In reality German weakness was concealed by bluff. **Questions 3–4**, however, remind pupils that there were calls to resist Hitler, although **Sources 13 and 14** are hindsight views. Finally, **question 5** asks pupils to synthesise sources to support a view. They might benefit from a template for this question. For each source, they should state:

- whether it indicates a French/British failure, a German success or a combination of both
- how they reached this conclusion
- the reliability of the source when checked against other sources and their own knowledge.

Why did Britain and France follow a policy of Appeasement?

Pupils who have studied the horrors of World War I might find it easier to grasp the reasons for Appeasement. However, these reasons are neatly summarised in the diagram on **page 216** and **questions 1 and 2** should provide pupils with the opportunity to show their understanding. Question 1 requires a straightforward summary of the source. However, a more in-depth look at the cartoon could provide useful ammunition for question 2. It would do no harm to remind pupils of their objectives for this question:

- To demonstrate their understanding of the policy and its origins
- To show recognition of the contemporary criticisms of the policy
- To acknowledge the widespread support for the policy at the time.

The Spanish Civil War

This is another short section, but it contains a number of crucial points which pupils need to absorb:

- Mussolini and Hitler ignoring the League's policy of non-intervention and trying out their new forces
- The advent of modern air warfare
- The helplessness of the League
- The Anti-Comintern Pact, bringing together the Fascist powers and presumably alarming the USSR.

This and previous sections are pulled together in the **Focus Task** on **page 217**. The failures of the League of Nations are well documented, and pupils will be familiar with them by now. They may not, however, have thought about the impact of these failures. The question is well suited to a piece of extended writing, but pupils might benefit from being provided with a structure (**Worksheet 8.3**).

Anschluss with Austria, 1938

As pupils reach this section they will probably feel the momentum towards war building up. Perhaps the key element in this section is the map, **Source 19**. Pupils should be able to see the true significance of the Anschluss in terms of the security of central Europe by looking at the spectre hovering over Czechoslovakia. This should complement **question 1** on **page 218**, which asks pupils to consider the Anschluss through the medium of cartoons. It might be useful to remind pupils of some criteria to use for testing cartoons:

Background

- The date it was drawn – what else was going on at the same time?
- The country and the type of publication in which the cartoon was published.

Words

- Look at the caption (if the cartoon has one) – it is usually very blunt.
- Many cartoons use labels on the characters or include objects. Look very carefully for these as they give very strong clues as to what the cartoon is about.

The cartoon itself

- Start by looking at the background if there is one – what sort of impression is it trying to give?
- Look at any figures and think about how the cartoonist has drawn them in terms of size, bulk and their position in relation to each other.
- Facial expressions are usually very important – they tell you whether the cartoonist thinks that a character is brave, cowardly, sincere, treacherous etc.

Pupils should also be prompted as to how they should make their judgements. The most useful cartoon will be relevant, informative and able to be placed in context. It may be that all three taken together provide the greatest value.

The Sudetenland, 1938

This key section covers the critical issues of the late 1930s:

- Was Appeasement the same policy in 1936 as it was in 1938?
- Was Hitler pursuing a master plan or was he gambling?
- Should we condemn or condone Appeasement?

Before introducing pupils to the controversy, the section stresses the general support enjoyed by Appeasement until early 1938. The **Activity** on **page 221** should help pupils to find their way through the intricate manoeuvrings. They might find it useful to try to represent these differing views on a timeline format, such as that laid out below.

Date	Event(s)	Chamberlain's view	Hitler's view	Beneš's view	Ordinary citizen's view
May 1938					

The controversy over Appeasement is raised in **questions 1–2** on **pages 220 and 221**. Pupils should spend time discussing these questions, as they will be able to use their work in the **Activity** on **page 222**. **Worksheet 8.4** provides some extra guidance on this.

The Nazi–Soviet Pact

It is sometimes difficult for pupils to grasp the horror and disappointment with which the Western Powers reacted to the announcement of the Nazi–Soviet Pact in 1939. This section therefore makes extensive use of primary source material to reinforce the story of the text. The aim is really to take pupils into the machinations and double dealing which constituted the pact.

Questions 1 and 2 on page 224 make use of a fairly clear message (**Source 33**) to get pupils to appreciate the Soviet position. In providing Stalin with a justification of Munich (question 2) they will appreciate Stalin's position further – he must have found any explanation unconvincing.

Questions 1 and 2 on page 225 ask pupils to cross-reference sources and text as they analyse the British viewpoint. This skill is exercised further in the remaining questions on this page, as pupils are asked to analyse, compare and contrast the views presented.

These contrasting views should help pupils to equip themselves for the **Activity** and the **Focus Tasks** on **pages 225 and 226**. The Activity is very much a review task, but with the emphasis on placing interpretations on events and their consequences. **Worksheet 8.5** provides a structure for this.

The **Focus Task** on Appeasement is similarly targeted and requires pupils to sift through material with a key issue in mind. The task demands some sophisticated thought processes, and pupils may need the support offered in **Worksheet 8.6**.

Some pupils might benefit from being given the relevant arguments and criticisms as a basis from which to work. For example:

Arguments in favour

- Memories of World War I
- Unfairness of some terms of Treaty of Versailles
- Widespread public support
- Buying time 1938–1939 for rearmament.

Arguments against

- Undermined the League of Nations
- Actually encouraged the dictators
- Violated the Treaty of Versailles
- Betrayed Czechoslovakia
- Forced Stalin to ally with Hitler.

The final **Focus Task** on **page 226** in this part of the chapter aims to take pupils into group work as preparation for a piece of extended writing. The process of sorting, categorising and linking sources is a powerful tool for understanding and using information rather than simply regurgitating it. The Focus Task is already highly structured, but there is a good deal of room for flexibility in such areas as group size and allocation of topics.

Part 2 HOW DID THE WAR BECOME A WORLD WAR?

This section is, in effect, a self-contained mini chapter, dealing with the origins of the war in the Pacific and the entry of the USA into the war against Germany. The narrative and the sources chart Roosevelt's change of mind over involvement in the war and the processes of preparing the American people for that eventuality.

The Focus Task on page 231 is designed to pull together these issues. Pupils might find it helpful to be given a set of prompts for the Roosevelt speech such as:

- The threat posed by Japan to the USA
- The potential consequences of German victory in Europe
- What Hitler said about the USA.

The response from Britain or Germany could be targeted at these points, supporting or contradicting them as appropriate.

WORKSHEET

8.1

The impact of the Treaty of Versailles

Below is a table which will help you organise your thoughts on the impact of the Treaty of Versailles. The important point about this table is that you can look over events at a glance. This means you must keep your entries short – use just a few notes and key words.

Terms of the Treaty of Versailles	What Hitler did and when	The reasons he gave for his actions	Response from Britain and France
Germany's armed forces to be severely limited			
Rhineland to be a demilitarised zone			
Germany forbidden to unite with Austria			
The Sudetenland taken in the new state of Czechoslovakia			
The Polish Corridor given to Poland			

WORKSHEET

Hitler's plans

8.2

AIM

To investigate Hitler's plans in the 1930s and how the British government might have interpreted them

RESOURCES

It is 1933. Write a briefing paper for the British government on Hitler's plans. Use Sources 3–5 on pages 210–211 to help you. You could set out your report like this:

Section 1
We have now looked at events in Germany and examined what the new leader, Hitler, may have in mind. The evidence available for this has been ...

Section 2
Taken at face value, some of Hitler's statements are worrying. In eastern Europe he plans ...

- _____
- _____
- _____

As far as western Europe is concerned ...

- _____
- _____
- _____

He also says a lot about the Treaty of Versailles ...

- _____
- _____
- _____

Section 3
There is a question about how serious Hitler is, and whether our evidence is totally reliable ...

- _____
- _____
- _____

Section 4
The British must consider their policies carefully. On the one hand, as a member of the League, Britain must _____

which means ...

- _____
- _____

On the other hand, a strong Communist government in the USSR means ...

- _____
- _____
- _____

The consequences of the failure of the League of Nations in the 1930s

AIM

To describe and explain how the failures of the League in the 1930s helped Hitler

RESOURCES

Look back over pages 199–209. Use the table below to decide how the failures of the League in the 1930s helped Hitler.

Failure of the League	Did it help Hitler directly?	Did it damage Hitler's opponents?	Did it create a situation which he could exploit?
Manchuria			
Disarmament			
Abyssinia			

EXTENSION WORK

'By failing to resist aggression in the 1930s, the League of Nations made Hitler's work easy.' How fair is this judgement on the actions of the League in the 1930s?

Organise your answer into paragraphs.
1 Your view (e.g. it is fair; it is not fair; it is partially fair)
2 Manchuria – how this event supports the judgement
3 Disarmament – how this event supports the judgement
4 Abyssinia – how this event supports the judgement
5 Balancing the argument – the League's problems
6 Your conclusion (e.g. more the League's fault than not).

WORKSHEET

8.4

Headline news, 30 September 1938

GCSE Modern World History

AIM

To use a range of sources to suggest what reactions to the Munich Agreement would have been

RESOURCES

Write a selection of newspaper headlines for 30 September 1938, the day after the Munich Agreement. Include the following in your selection:

1 Different British newspapers (Clues: pro- and anti-Appeasement; Sources 27–29, page 222)
2 A neutral American newspaper (A neutral view?)
3 A German newspaper (Note: all German newspapers were under Nazi control by 1938)
4 A Czech newspaper (See pages 219–221)
5 A Polish newspaper

For each headline, decide whether it will view Munich as a triumph or a sell-out.

EXTENSION WORK

Choose one of the headlines and write a short article to go with it.
Make sure it supports your headline.
Find quotations, cartoons and maps which support your view from pages 218–222.

The Second World War – Hitler's war?

8.5

AIM

To investigate the extent to which Hitler alone was responsible for the Second World War

RESOURCES

Imagine that Hitler is on trial. He is facing the charge that he deliberately planned and started the Second World War.

The trial begins with a summary of events.

Hitler's actions

Date	Action
1933	Took Germany out of the League of Nations
1934	Tried to take over Austria but was prevented by Mussolini
1935	Held massive rearmament rally in Germany
1936	Reintroduced conscription in Germany
1937	Tried out Germany's new weapons in the Spanish Civil War
1938	Took over Austria
	Took over the Sudetenland area of Czechoslovakia
1939	Invaded the rest of Czechoslovakia
	Invaded Poland
	War

Your task

1 Once you have looked at the summary of events, draw up three columns on a sheet of paper:

Factors for which Hitler was totally responsible	Factors for which he was partly responsible	Factors not connected to Hitler

2 Decide how the prosecution would make use of your lists.

- Which seem to support the charge that it was all planned?
- What supporting examples and evidence would they use?

3 Now explain how the defence would use the above events. Remember, the defence is not trying to prove Hitler innocent. They are simply trying to show that he did not plan the war. They might therefore argue that Hitler thought the French and British secretly approved of some of his actions. 'The failure of the League showed that international relations were not about co-operation but every man for himself.'

4 Look back over your answers to 2 and 3. Which is more convincing?

Was Appeasement justified?

8.6

AIM

To examine the evidence for differing interpretations of the policy of Appeasement

RESOURCES

Your task is to prepare a balanced answer to the question above, pointing out the strengths and weaknesses of the policy of Appeasement.

Here is one view on the issue:

Those who are ready to fight whenever some challenge comes from a foreign power, have not always been right. On the other hand, those whose inclination is to bow their heads to seek patiently and faithfully for peaceful compromise are not always wrong.

(Winston Churchill commenting after the Second World War on the policy of Appeasement. Winston Churchill is famous as a fierce critic of Appeasement but this source shows him taking a more balanced view.)

Your task is to come up with your own view. Work in stages.

1 Look back through pages 216–225 for evidence which seems to justify Appeasement.

Arguments for Appeasement	Evidence to support the arguments

2 Look back through pages 216–225 for evidence which seems to support the criticisms of Appeasement.

Criticisms of Appeasement	Evidence to support the criticisms

3 Now explain your own views in paragraphs:

Paragraph 1: Winston Churchill expressed this view on Appeasement …
My opinion of his view is …
Paragraph 2: Appeasement can certainly be criticised because …
Paragraph 3: On the other hand, supporters of Appeasement believed …
Paragraph 4: On balance, therefore, I believe …

The Second World War
What kind of war was it?

Key features of the chapter

	Issue covered	Assessment elements	Format(s) for pupil work
Focus Task (p.234): Timeline of World War II	Chronology of World War II	Analysing key events	Timeline and written summary
Activity (p.237): Warfare	Aspects of warfare from World War I to World War II	Analysing and describing change	Written report
Activity (p.239): Never Again	Horrors of World War II	Using sources	Designing posters

This short chapter aims simply to show the scale of this truly world war. As such its implications were enormous. The chapter establishes a context for the post-war chapters.

The course of the war is set out in a series of annotated maps. To show their understanding of key events, pupils are asked in the **Focus Task** on **page 234** to draw up a timeline. This could be a single timeline amalgamating all the main events, or three separate ones. If the latter option is chosen, the timelines should be on the same sheet to allow pupils an overview. Similarly, the explanatory sentences in Part 2 of the task might be added as annotations on the timeline, if space permits.

For **question 1** on **page 235**, the details of the photographs are as follows:

A British tanks advance: El Alamein
B US troops clearing Japanese snipers: Gilbert Islands, November 1943
C Finnish ski patrol attacking Russian troops
D Winter convoy, 23 December 1940
E Servicemen in Europe

How was this war different?

This question is addressed entirely through visual and statistical sources, effecting a comparison between the Great War and the war of 1939–1945. The **Activity** should stimulate a lively and enjoyable discussion, at the same time exercising pupils' ability to extract information from visual sources. The Activity would also lend itself very readily to extended research using a range of other source materials.

How did the war affect civilians?

Again, there is a strong emphasis on the visual in this section. This is particularly relevant to the **Activity** on **page 239** in which pupils have to demonstrate their understanding through the medium of a poster. They should not find much difficulty in developing poster ideas under the theme 'Never Again'. **Worksheet 9.1** should help them construct their poster.

The nuclear age

This final section is in many respects the most important. For the next chapter, pupils should make themselves thoroughly familiar with the changes outlined in **Source 24**. **Worksheet 9.2** provides a reduced version of Source 24, around which they can record what they see as key changes.

The effects of the Second World War

9.1

GCSE Modern World History

AIM

To demonstrate understanding of the impact of the Second World War

RESOURCES

It is the end of the war. You have been commissioned by the UNO to make a poster about the Second World War using the title 'Never Again'.

To get you thinking make notes in each of these boxes.

Step 3
In this box, list what images could be in your poster.

Step 1
In this box note down all of the effects of the war which you can see on pages 238–239.

Step 2
In this box make a note of what you are trying to achieve with this poster.

Step 4
In this box try out different slogans for your poster.

WORKSHEET

A new world?

9.2

AIM

To record the changes brought about by the Second World War

RESOURCES

1 Put the effects of the Second World War shown in the diagram into order of importance by writing 1, 2, 3 or 4 next to each.

2 Draw up a table like the one below and explain why you have put the effects in the positions you have.

Position	Effect	Why it has this position
1		
2		

In many European countries the old pre-war leaders were swept aside, particularly those who were thought to have helped the Germans. In France, Scandinavia and the Balkans the resistance leaders were seen as the natural leaders of the country after the war.

The war gave a real boost to independence movements in colonies owned by European countries. Within three years India had been granted independence from Britain. Twenty years after the war Britain had lost almost all its empire.

The war crippled the economies of the European powers. Economic recovery was even more difficult than after the First World War. This actually strengthened the will to co-operate and over the following twenty years led to the setting up of the first stages of the European Union.

The war had shown that the two most powerful countries in the world were the capitalist USA and the Communist USSR. In the war they had been allies against Germany and Japan. The question was whether they would get on after the war. Would the friendship hold? You can find out all about that in Chapter 10.

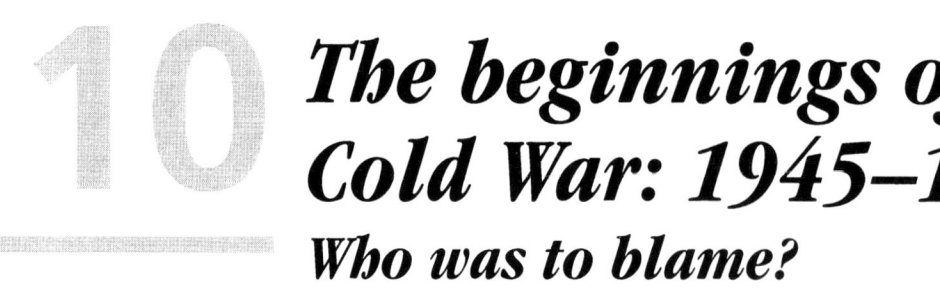

The beginnings of the Cold War: 1945–1948
Who was to blame?

Key features of the chapter

	Issue covered	Assessment elements	Format(s) for pupil work
Focus Task (p.246): Yalta	Behind the scenes at Yalta	Use of sources	Assessing evidence, follow-up written work
Focus Task (p.249): Relations 1945+	Why did the Allies begin to fall out after 1945?	Selecting and organising knowledge	Note-taking
Focus Task (p.253): Eastern Europe	How did the USSR gain control of eastern Europe?	Selecting and organising historical knowledge, sources	Report to Truman
Focus Task (p.256): USA–USSR	How did the USA react to Soviet expansion?	Changes, key features of historical situation, sources	Report to Stalin
Focus Task (p.260): Cold War	When did the Cold War start?	Selecting and organising knowledge	Discussion/report
Focus Task (p.261): Cold War responsibility	Who was to blame for the Cold War?	Use of sources, analysing and explaining events	Extended writing

The Yalta Conference: February 1945 – the Issue Starter

The Yalta Conference is an ideal issue starter for the topic. The contrasts between the outward smiles and handshakes and the behind-the-scenes doubts should help pupils appreciate that the history of this period is a 'two-track' history with a discrepancy between the public and the private.

Question 1 on page 245 directs pupils straight to the first of these two tracks. It merits a written response, perhaps after a short class discussion. The aim is to establish that, in principle, the powers were looking at mechanisms for peace and security in Europe. Teachers will probably find it worthwhile to stress to pupils the agreement over eastern Europe becoming a Soviet sphere of influence as this issue will be raised later.

The **Focus Task** on **pages 246–247** immediately presents pupils with a contrasting view (the other track) to that presented on page 245. **Worksheet 10.1** provides a framework within which pupils can interpret and marshal the evidence. The worksheet also includes suggestions for extension work and support for that work.

The **Activity** on **page 247** could be usefully employed as a checking device. Press releases should be brief – 100 words at most. Through this device pupils can show succinctly whether or not they have grasped the issue of the twin-track history of the period.

The Potsdam Conference: July–August 1945

In this section the second track uncovered by the pupils at Yalta becomes more apparent. The photograph of the handshake is a powerful image and is worth some consideration. **Questions 2–4** at the foot of **page 248** raise extremely important issues. They could be addressed either as written or discussion exercises. The key point is for pupils to recognise that they are witnessing the beginnings of a clash of two entirely different philosophies.

This is considered in greater depth in the **Focus Task** on **page 249**. **Worksheet 10.2** provides a pro forma for pupils to organise their thoughts. Perhaps the most effective procedure would be for pupils to use the worksheet as a first try. After a teacher-led feedback session they could write up a final version in their files or exercise books.

The emphasis of the section now begins to shift towards eastern Europe and the 'internal' Communist takeovers. **Source 18** attempts to show pupils at a glance the extent of territory and population gained by Communists immediately after the war. **Questions 1–4** on **pages 250–251** require written responses and ask pupils to comprehend sources in context. Questions 1 and 2 necessitate careful scrutiny of Source 18. Pupils should be encouraged to categorise these factors and 'slot in' examples under the headings. This should discourage copying. The comparison of the disparate views of **Sources 16 and 17** should impress upon pupils the irreconcilable positions emerging in 1946. The key point for them to grasp is that both sides felt that they held entirely justifiable positions.

The Cold War

This section builds on pupils' recognition of these entrenched positions. **Question 3** on **page 251** introduces pupils to the concept of the Cold War. **Source 21** and the **Factfiles** on **page 252** look backwards to explore the possibility that such a conflict was highly likely and that Hitler simply delayed it.

Question 1 on page 252 explores the contrast between the two systems. Pupils should find the process of annotating the diagrams with details from the Factfiles a useful exercise, and it should provide them with a handy revision tool. **Questions 2 and 3** should see pupils both targeting the overt differences between the two systems and beginning to appreciate that there are different interpretations of ideas such as the good of the people.

The **Focus Task** on **page 253** focuses attention on the thorny question of eastern Europe and what the American response to Stalin's takeover should be. The task itself is structured into four main sections. Some pupils may benefit from being directed to particular resources or sections of text to locate the necessary information. However, by attempting the preceding questions, pupils should be in a position to interpret and apply what they have already learned, rather than searching extensively for new material.

The reaction of the West

This section tries to take pupils behind the obvious fact that the Americans began to oppose Soviet expansion in Europe. **Question 1** on **page 254** requires an analysis both of the message and context of the two sources. Applying the usual criteria for looking at cartoons (see page 50) should enable pupils to tackle this without excessive difficulty.

Question 2 on page 255 exercises similar skills but requires a good deal more in the way of lateral thinking. Pupils must understand the link, in American eyes, between poverty and Communism. This understanding, along with **Source 25** and the section on the Truman Doctrine, should give pupils the necessary raw material for the poster **Activity** on **page 255**.

An effective extension exercise is to ask pupils to explain why their poster looks the way it does and how it is meant to achieve its ends.

Marshall Aid receives in-depth treatment and in **questions 1–3** on **page 256** pupils should be set thinking about the relationship between Marshall Aid and the Truman Doctrine. For question 1 they should try to be as concise as possible in identifying political and economic factors. The key process is that of drawing the connecting lines, and above all justifying those lines. **Worksheet 10.3** provides a format for this.

Sources 27–29 broaden the issue by providing pupils with contemporary views of Marshall Aid. By applying the criteria mentioned earlier, pupils should be able to work out the (sometimes) subtle messages contained within them.

All of this work should prepare pupils for the **Focus Task** on **page 256**, the report for Stalin. As in the corresponding report for Truman, the task is clearly structured. Some pupils may again benefit from being given precise page and source references to help them locate relevant information. However, the aim is above all to process information and show understanding.

Why did the Soviet Union blockade Berlin?

After much scene setting, this section covers the first overt superpower confrontation. As well as dealing with the events in their own right, the section tries to establish the blockade as part of the context of the developing Cold War.

Questions 1 and 2 on page 258 introduce pupils to the culture of accusation and counter-accusation. This is developed in the next three questions, which stress the importance of differing interpretations. Pupils should be encouraged in the final two questions to 'fudge' their answers. Thus, rather than opting for one source, they might explain why some combination, when used in a certain way, would be of greatest value.

Why was NATO set up? / A divided Germany

These two short sections essentially set out some of the short-term consequences of the Berlin Blockade. The pivotal position of Berlin in the coming Cold War is established and **questions 6 and 7** on **page 259** should allow pupils to see the lines drawn for this war.

A pattern for the Cold War

Clearly the key elements of this section are the two **Focus Tasks**. The first task, which looks at the starting date of the Cold War, could be tackled in various ways. Clearly there is no right answer and it is the process of discussion which is beneficial. The main processes are:

- To define Cold War with a set of criteria such as conflicting ideologies; use of propaganda; working through other parties
- To evaluate the 'claims' of key events to be the starting point of the Cold War
- To reach a substantiated conclusion.

Worksheet 10.4 provides a framework which aims to guide pupils through the information and concepts, but which is clearly focused on these objectives.

The **Focus Task** on **page 261** focuses on the blame attributable to the USA and the USSR. Some historians would agree that this is simplistic and that Britain itself should bear as much blame as the USA and the USSR. We have not included this option as it is not a syllabus focus point.

WORKSHEET

10.1

The Yalta Conference 1945

The war against Hitler brought Roosevelt, Stalin and Churchill together and at the Yalta Conference they seemed to get on well. But what was going on behind the scenes?

1 Study Sources 2–11 on pages 246–247 carefully and complete the table below.

Remember:

• Your aim is to search for evidence of agreement or disagreement between the Allies.
• You must also consider the reliability of the sources.

AIM

To use and evaluate a range of sources to investigate events behind the scenes at the Yalta Conference

RESOURCES

Source	Evidence of disagreement between the Allies?	Evidence of agreement ?	Your views on the reliability of the source
2			
3			
4			
5			
6			
7			
8			
9			
10			
11			

EXTENSION WORK

Look at Source 1 on page 245 and then answer the question below.

'Source 1 presents a picture of friendship and trust between the Big Three. However, a close look at other evidence suggests that this picture does not tell the whole story.' Explain this statement.

You need to answer this question in paragraphs:

Paragraph 1: Source 1 is certainly not useless as a view of Yalta. We know that the Big Three reached a number of important agreements. For example …

Paragraph 2: However, some evidence seems to suggest that Stalin had his suspicions about his allies. For example …
Of course, we must treat this evidence with care because …

Paragraph 3: Churchill and Roosevelt were also suspicious of Stalin. We know this from …
Again we must take care because …

Paragraph 4: There also seems to be evidence of a personality clash between Stalin and Churchill. For example …

Paragraph 5: In conclusion, therefore, I would like to point out that I feel the statement is basically correct because …

WORKSHEET

10.2

Why did the Allies begin to fall out in 1945?

AIM

To examine the relative importance of different reasons why relations turned sour in 1945

RESOURCES

Read carefully through pages 248–249, looking at text and sources. Your job is to look out for evidence of why relations between the Big Three got worse. Organise your evidence under three headings:

• **Clash of personalities**
(What changes since Yalta? Evidence that personalities caused clashes?)

• **Actions of the USA**
(Evidence that US actions upset Stalin; USA's views on this)

• **Actions of the USSR**
(Evidence that USSR's actions upset Truman and the UK; Stalin's views on this)

When you have finished the chart, compare it with others in your class.
If there are any differences, explain to each other why there are.
If you think you need to, reorganise your chart so that you feel happy with it.

Clash of personalities	Actions of the USA	Actions of the USSR

EXTENSION WORK

Write a short report of about 200 words maximum with the title 'Why did the Allies begin to fall out in 1945?'.

WORKSHEET

10.3

Marshall Aid

1 Read through pages 255–256, which cover Marshall Aid. Look for the aims of Marshall Aid. When you find an aim, decide whether it is mainly a political or economic reason and put it in the correct section.

2 Now look at your finished diagram. Decide which aims are connected and draw lines between them. Either write explanations on the lines, or use a key and explain the lines in your file or exercise book.

Economic aims

MARSHALL AID

Political aims

AIM

To explain why the USA introduced Marshall Aid

RESOURCES

WORKSHEET

When did the Cold War begin?

10.4

To analyse and explain why it is difficult to explain when the Cold War began

When did the Cold War begin? There is no right answer to this question and different historians have their own views. Your task is to look at why it is so difficult to decide.

Step 1

Look at this definition of the Cold War.
'A Cold War has the following characteristics:

1 Conflicting ideologies (political ideas)
2 Arguments between leaders
3 Use of propaganda and the media
4 Build-up of arms
5 Working through other groups or countries against the opponent.'

Are you happy with this definition? If not, add other characteristics to the list.

Step 2

Now look at these events and use the table to see whether they fit the definition.

Event / Characteristic	1	2	3	4	5	Others
Yalta Conference						
Potsdam						
Communist takeover in eastern Europe						
Czechoslovakia						
Greece						
Marshall Aid						
Truman Doctrine						
Berlin Blockade						
NATO						

Step 3

Now write a series of paragraphs explaining why it is difficult to say when the Cold War began.

Paragraph 1: I would define a Cold War as …

_____

However, it is difficult to identify a starting point because …

_____

Paragraph 2: The Yalta and Potsdam Conferences partly fit this definition because …

_____

However, some features are missing at this stage. For example …

_____

Paragraph 3: Other events also fit the definition to some extent.
For example …

_____

Paragraph 4: However, all of these elements seem to be in place by the time of …

_____

Paragraph 5: Therefore, I conclude that the Cold War was definitely under way by …
However, it is much harder to say exactly when it began because …

_____

WORKSHEET

10.5

Who was to blame for the Cold War?

AIM

To investigate different possible interpretations of the causes of the Cold War

RESOURCES

In small groups, ideally of five, investigate who was to blame for the Cold War. The possible verdicts are:

1 USA was most to blame.
2 USSR was most to blame.
3 Both sides were equally to blame.
4 No one was to blame. The Cold War was inevitable.

Step 1

In your group, find out whether one verdict is most popular.

Step 2

Now divide a number of factors between you:

- Personal relationships between the leaders (pages 244–251)
- The conflicting beliefs of the superpowers (pages 245–253)
- War damage suffered by the USSR (pages 245–259)
- Stalin's takeover of eastern Europe (pages 248–250)
- Marshall Aid for Europe (pages 255–256)

(You may be able to find more information in other books or on computer files.)

Report back to your group using a table like this:

Factor	Examples	Supports which verdict?	Reason

Step 3

Now, as a group, decide which verdict the evidence seems to support.

Step 4

Explain your final verdict in a series of paragraphs.

Paragraph 1: (a) State the evidence for and against Verdict 1.
(b) Explain why, after considering the evidence, you accept/reject the verdict.

Repeat this process for Verdicts 2–4.
Finish with your conclusion.

Key features of the chapter

	Issue(s) covered	Assessment elements	Format(s) for pupil work
Focus Task (p.268): China 1949	Why did China become a Communist state?	Selecting and deploying information	Extended writing (report)
Focus Task (p.269): Chinese agriculture	How did agriculture change?	Selection and deploying information, describing change	Speech (notes)
Focus Task (p.273): Communist reforms	What was the impact of the Communist reforms?	Analysing and describing change	Written report
Focus Task (p.275): Communist rule	Did Chinese people benefit from Communist rule?	Use of sources, selecting and deploying information	Comparisons
Focus Task (p.278): The Cultural Revolution	Causes and consequences of the Cultural Revolution	Use of sources, selecting and deploying information	Written report, discussion
Focus Task (p.278): Mao's dictatorship	Did Mao create a cruel dictatorship?	Use of sources, selecting and employing information	Substantiated writing
Focus Task (p.283): China and the USA	Why did China try to improve relations with the USA?	Use of sources	Supported explanation
Focus Task (p.283): China and the world	Was China a superpower by 1976?	Use of sources	Diagram and explanation
Focus Task (p.283): Foreign relations	How have foreign relations improved since Mao's death?	Describing and analysing change	Diagram and extended writing

Part 1 DID COMMUNISM MAKE CHINA A FAIRER COUNTRY?

The Issue Starter

An ideal issue starter for the chapter could be **Source 4** on **page 264**. Pupils could have to deal with a range of questions, such as

- Have they heard of Mao?
- Why should a march be important?
- What do they understand by the term 'civil war'?

This brief analysis would introduce them to several of the key features of China's history:

- Internal dissension
- China's vast size and population
- The determination of Mao.

How did the Communists win the Civil War?

This section opens with other important features of China's history – foreign intervention and its ancient culture. Pupils gain valuable background knowledge about China's situation in the early twentieth century. The **Factfile** and narrative should give them enough information to appreciate fully the significance of the Long March, particularly after reading **Source 5**.

The war against Japan

The Japanese invasion is inextricable from the Civil War and the eventual victory of the Communists over the Nationalists. **Questions 1–5** on **pages 264 and 265** should help pupils understand how the Communists were able to survive in the face of enormous odds and the enmity of both Nationalists and the Japanese. The questions are 'intermediaries' – their main purpose is to ensure careful reading. However, questions 4 and 5 require some analysis of the sources.

Questions 1–4 on pages 266–267 should further enhance pupils' understanding of the Communist victory. Questions 1 and 2 require them to comprehend sources but also to be aware of their context. Questions 3 and 4 certainly require formal written answers. Together, they introduce pupils to the fundamentals of a kind of warfare which was to prove hugely successful in Vietnam, Afghanistan and many other world trouble spots in later years of the twentieth century.

The impact of this and other factors is pulled together in the **Focus Task** on **page 268**. Pupils might find the framework on **Worksheet 11.1** helpful in structuring their work. The essence of the task is that they show their understanding of key causal factors.

China under the Communists 1949–1965

The changes brought about by the Communists once peace was established must have seemed remarkable. This next section focuses on the Communist reforms and their impact on the Chinese people. The **Focus Task** on **page 269** asks pupils to evaluate the impact of the Communists' reforms in agriculture. The format of the task could be changed to a simple written report. However, the speech format retains the elements of advocacy and interpretation. In addition, pupils may be motivated (or threatened!) by the prospect of delivering the speech from their own notes, or even those of other pupils. **Worksheet 11.2** provides a structure to help pupils plan and present their work.

The section then moves on to deal with the attempts to build up industry in China throughout the Five-Year Plans. **Questions 1 and 2** on **page 270** raise extremely important issues. The **Activity** on **page 271** should help pupils to understand the enormity of the task of turning China into an industrial superpower. Similarly, **question 3** asks pupils to consider why Mao wanted to sweep away the old order of Chinese society, and look at the kind of society he did want.

There might well be time for some profitable speculative discussion between pupils and teacher at this point:

- Was it wise to attempt such sweeping reforms?
- How would ordinary people react?
- Which reforms seemed more likely to succeed?
- What do they know of China today? Does that throw any light on the situation?

Implicit in these discussions will be that such revolutionary upheavals require great discipline if they are to be managed effectively. This should take pupils neatly into the subsection on control. In comparison with the brutality of the early Communist period in Russia, Communist control in China might appear rather tame. However, pupils should try to understand the vast scale of the propaganda campaign and the enormous pressure brought to bear on some sections of Chinese society.

This pressure, and indeed the benefits for some under the Communists, can be brought to the fore by pupils in the **Focus Task** on **page 273**. As well as the straightforward merits and demerits of Communist rule, pupils should try to pick up the less tangible 'atmosphere' of China under the Communists. The example of Mao's war on sparrows is a good example of the absurd exemplifying the serious.

This 'atmosphere' is dealt with on **pages 274–275**. The Hundred Flowers remains something of a puzzle to historians, and **question 1** on **page 274** allows pupils to speculate for themselves. **Question 2** on **Source 26** is equally important, making a link with the questions on **page 275** on the Great Leap Forward. Using **Sources 27–30** pupils should begin to form views on the following issues:

- The true motives for the Great Leap Forward
- The real, as opposed to propaganda, achievements
- The split with the USSR.

The **Focus Task** on **page 275** asks pupils to dig beneath the issues and power struggles in the Party to look at the lives of ordinary Chinese. **Worksheet 11.3** provides support for pupils for their research and presentation.

The Cultural Revolution

The Cultural Revolution, with its focus on young people, is usually of great interest. This section uses an array of sources alongside the narrative text to introduce pupils to the main issues. **Question 1** on **page 277** asks pupils to assess the aims of the Revolution and the methods used. Teachers will scarcely need reminding to take care over the use of the term 'notes'. This can often be taken as a euphemism for copying, unless stringent guidelines are set, such as word limits, or a prescribed layout. The **Focus Task** at the top of **page 278** addresses the two key issues of why Mao began the Cultural Revolution and its consequences. The task is sufficiently structured for all pupils, although some might wish to draw up a table format to help them organise their own ideas.

The death of Mao

This section attempts to assess Mao's legacy. It also provides the location for the **Focus Task** asking pupils to attempt a more detailed evaluation of his role in Chinese history. **Worksheet 11.4** provides a framework for the task.

China after the death of Mao

This final, short section should give pupils an added perspective on China and Mao after the Focus Task. The brutal crushing of the Tiananmen Square demonstrations continues to haunt China. **Questions 1–4** on **page 279** allow pupils to draw out the relevant information fairly readily. They are also designed (questions 3 and 4 in particular) to allow them to come to their own conclusions on the nature of the post-Mao regime.

Part 2 WHAT WAS COMMUNIST CHINA'S IMPACT ON THE WIDER WORLD?

China and its neighbours

The aim of the questions on **page 280** is that pupils look closely at **Source 1** and recognise some fundamental changes which have taken place since the Communist takeover. After 1949 China was no longer a disunited and victimised state. This changing status is amply demonstrated by the hostile American reaction, in the UNO and in general, to the Communist success.

China and the superpowers

Pupils will probably benefit from knowing that the true significance of China in the global balance is perhaps not fully understood today, and is far from being agreed upon. **Sources 2 and 6** illustrate the determination of Mao to be his own man and his willingness to oppose openly both the USA and USSR.

Sources 4–7 on page 282 are clearly directed towards the first **Focus Task** on **page 283**. The task concentrates on analysing and combining the sources to find reasons for improving relations. As an extension exercise, pupils could be asked to identify links between the reasons as well as identifying what they believe to be the most important factor. **Worksheet 11.5** provides a framework for this.

The second **Focus Task** on **page 283** addresses the thorny issue of whether China was a superpower by 1976. The task is structured to allow all pupils to tackle it. However, teachers could provide a structure which is broken down further still. The emphasis is on pupils looking back through their work as well as the book, and applying a set of criteria. Thus a recording grid, with sources down the left and how they match the criteria along the top of the grid, would enable pupils to gain an all-important overview.

The chapter closes with a **Focus Task** dealing with relations since Mao's death. Again, the emphasis is on review and overview and the instructions should prove straightforward. Pupils may be able to use CD-ROM or other reference tools to locate actual headlines. The choice and explanation of a turning point could provide a basis for a lively and fruitful discussion.

WORSHEET *Why did China become a Communist state?*

11.1

GCSE Modern World History

AIM

To describe and explain the main reasons for the Communist victory

RESOURCES

Write a report to explain why China became Communist in 1949.

Step 1

Use the table below to note down key points and ideas for your report.

Impact of war on Nationalists	Impact of war on Communists	Relations between peasants and Communists	Communist tactics against Nationalists

Step 2

Now organise your findings and write your report in paragraphs:

1 How the Second World War weakened the Nationalists
2 How it strengthened the Communists
3 Why the Communists gained support from the peasants
4 Why the Communists were successful in the Civil War

How did agriculture change under the Communists?

AIM

To describe and explain why changes in agriculture brought about by the Communists were generally successful

RESOURCES

Your task

Prepare notes for a speech to be given by Chairman Mao in 1957. Mao wishes to make the following points:

1 Many people said the peasants would resist change but they were wrong.
2 Although results have varied, the changes have generally been successful.

Mao does not want to read out his speech; he simply wants some notes as reminders of what he is planning to say. Provide the points he needs on the cue cards.

CHINESE FARMING BEFORE 1949

Point: _____

_____

Evidence to show Mao was right:

_____
_____
_____
_____

HOW PEASANTS DEALT WITH THE LANDLORDS

Point: _____

_____

Evidence to show Mao was right:

_____
_____
_____

HOW FARMING METHODS CHANGED

Point: _____

_____

Evidence to show Mao was right:

_____
_____
_____
_____

WHETHER ATTITUDES SEEM TO HAVE CHANGED

Point: _____

_____

Evidence to show Mao was right:

_____
_____
_____

WHETHER THE CHANGES WERE SUCCESSFUL

Point: _____

_____

Evidence to show Mao was right:

_____
_____
_____

WORKSHEET

11.3

Did Chinese people benefit from Communist rule?

AIM

To analyse the impact of the changes brought by the Communists on the lives of ordinary Chinese

RESOURCES

Step 1

Look back over pages 268–275 and fill in the table below. You may work in pairs, one of you looking for benefits, the other for hardships caused by the Communists.

Benefits brought by Communists	Hardships brought by Communists

Step 2

In each column, use a different ink, pencil or highlighter pen to indicate things which happened to different groups (e.g. peasants in blue ink; merchants in red ink; landlords ...)

Step 3

Now answer the question below in paragraphs:

Did Chinese people benefit from Communist rule?

Paragraph 1: There were certainly groups in China who did benefit from Communist rule. These were the ... They benefited by ...

Paragraph 2: However, there were also those who suffered. For example ...
They suffered in the following ways ...

Paragraph 4: There were also groups who both gained and lost in different ways. For example ...

Paragraph 4: My conclusion, therefore, is ...

Did Mao create a cruel dictatorship in China?

AIM

To examine the impact of Mao on the way in which China was governed

RESOURCES

Read Source 40 on page 278 of your textbook. Now imagine Mao is on trial. He is accused of creating a cruel dictatorship in China and Source 40 is a key piece of evidence against him.

You may wish to work in pairs, one gathering evidence for the defence, the other for the prosecution.

The defence

Look back over your work on this period and at pages 268–278. Then complete this table, giving a summary of Mao's achievements.

Problems facing Mao when he took over	Legacy of Japanese occupation	Achievements of the 1950s

The prosecution

Use this table to record evidence which you can present at the trial to show Mao's mistakes and cruelty.

Communist methods	Mao's mistakes	The Cultural Revolution

Summary

Now use your findings to write a balanced view of the question:

Did Mao create a cruel dictatorship in China?

Paragraph 1: Your balanced view (he did; he did not; he did to some extent)
Paragraph 2: Positive contributions made by Mao (with evidence)
Paragraph 3: Criticisms of Mao (with evidence)
Paragraph 4: How you reached your view (explain which pieces of evidence help you form your view).

Why did China try to improve relations with the USA?

AIM

To use a range of sources to explain why China tried to improve its relations with the USA

RESOURCES

1 Study Sources 4–7 on page 282 carefully and then complete the chart below.

Source 4	Suggests reason(s) for better relations is/are:
	• _____

• _____

• _____

This links with the view in Source(s)

• _____

• _____

Source 5	Suggests reason(s) for better relations is/are:
	• _____

• _____

• _____

This links with the view in Source(s)

• _____

• _____

Source 6	Suggests reason(s) for better relations is/are:
	• _____

• _____

• _____

This links with the view in Source(s)

• _____

• _____

Source 7	
	Suggests reason(s) for better relations is/are:
	• _____

• _____

• _____

This links with the view in Source(s)

• _____

• _____

2 Explain which of the reasons you believe is the most important.

3 Choose two reasons which you believe to be linked. Explain how they are linked.

12

The Cold War 1950–1973
Did the USA manage to contain the spread of Communism?

Key features of the chapter

	Issue covered	Assessment elements	Format(s) for pupil work
Activity (p.289): Korea	Truman's view on his dismissal	Key features of historical situation	Letter to Truman
Focus Task (p.290): Korean War	Was the Korean War a success for containment?	Selecting and deploying knowledge, describe and explain events	Report to President
Activity (p.295): Cuban crisis 1962	Options open to Kennedy	Describing and explaining events	Report to President
Focus Task (p.298): Cuba 1962	The Cuban missile crisis: a success for containment?	Use of sources, analysing events	Structured writing
Focus Task (p.300): Vietnam	Why did the Americans get involved in Vietnam?	Use of sources, analysing events	Report
Focus Task (p.305): Vietnam	Why did the USA lose the Vietnam War?	Selecting and deploying knowledge	Structured writing
Focus Task (p.305): Containment	How successful was the policy of containment?	Selecting and deploying knowledge	Case-study comparison

Anti-Communism in the USA – the Issue Starter

McCarthyism provides an excellent issue starter. Through it pupils should be able to appreciate the true depth of anti-Communist paranoia in some circles of American society. **Questions 1 and 2** on **page 286** guide pupils towards an analysis of this unpleasant spirit. Pupils will need to analyse the elements of each of **Sources 1–4** but also place them in the context of the USA in the early years of the Cold War. The ideal format would probably be a short discussion leading to written answers. The questions do invite some interesting speculation:

- Was this the mood of all of the USA?
- How could we investigate this question?

Case-study 1: The Korean War

The chapter pulls out three case studies of containment in action, the first of which is Korea. Pupils need to be reminded that there are a number of issues to bear in mind as they tackle the study:

- The 'umbrella' issue of containment
- Comparisons between this and other Cold War confrontations
- The position of the UNO.

Question 1 on page 288 deals with the background but tries to get pupils into an analysis of US pressure for UN intervention. The Russian boycott over China is an essential point in the context of Korea and in terms of setting the scene for future clashes in the UNO. By examining MacArthur closely, pupils should gain a perspective on the ongoing issues outlined above. The position of the UNO is addressed further in **question 3**. The question demands a straightforward *comprehension* of the sources, but an *evaluation* of the sources would be entirely appropriate, even if it did not have a great effect on pupils' views.

The dismissal of MacArthur is a dramatic incident and the **Activity** on **page 289** offers much opportunity for pupils to explore it. Some pupils might benefit from a few prompts for their letter such as:

- What he believed his mission to be
- Why he felt containment was right
- Why North Korea should be conquered
- Why he did not believe the Chinese were such a great threat.

A framework for the letter is set out in **Worksheet 12.1**.

Pupils' understanding of the Korean War in the context of containment is then tested in the **Focus Task** on **page 290**. Pupils must employ a range of skills. **Worksheets 12.2a and 12.2b** both support this task. 12.2(a) is a framework for studying all three case-studies in this chapter and for reaching a judgement on the policy of containment as a whole. Pupils should therefore complete the relevant section on Korea and then keep the sheet safe, coming back to it after studying Cuba and Vietnam.

The second part of the Focus Task concentrates on containment in the context of the Korean War and Worksheet 12.2b provides support for this. The section continues to deal with the theme of containment and how it was pursued into the 1950s. **Questions 1 and 2** on **page 291** merit written answers and should sharpen pupils' understanding of this more aggressive form of containment.

The arms race

A parallel issue, and one which is closely related, is introduced by the visual sources at the top of **page 292**. As well as being a topic of major importance, this focus on the arms race does of course set the scene for the Cuban missile crisis. **Questions 1–3** are perhaps best addressed in a discussion format where the full range of possibilities can be explored. The position of US missiles in Europe should be stressed particularly strongly, as they form an obvious counterpoint to missiles in Cuba. Questions 2 and 3 are 'intermediary' questions, containing important points of perspective for studying Cuba.

Question 1 on page 292 develops the emphasis on cartoons in this chapter. The emphasis is very much on analysis, provenance and context. The formula used for analysing cartoons should be readily usable in this context. Also, **Worksheet 12.3** provides an opportunity to view a series of cartoons and the way in which they reflect the period.

Case-study 2: The Cuban missile crisis

This dramatic and gripping episode is perhaps the most tense of Cold War confrontations. **Questions 5–7** on **page 293** require written responses, as they give pupils some important background information. The proximity of Cuba to the USA is, of course, the key point for pupils to grasp.

Question 8 asks pupils to comprehend sources, but also reminds them of the umbrella theme of containment. **Question 1** on **page 294** should reinforce pupils' overview, by asking them to look back across several pages and compare the situation of the USA's missiles in Europe with those of the USSR in Cuba.

Pupils can probably sympathise with the young President Kennedy, and the **Activity** on **page 295** gives them a structure for evaluating the options open to him. The Activity could readily be carried out as a small-group discussion exercise. **Worksheet 12.4** provides a structure to be used either as a planning tool for a discussion or debate, or to be written up.

Questions 1 and 2 on page 296 bring pupils back to the story and are suitable for dealing with in discussion. This leads logically on to questions 3 and 4, centred on the seminal Source 27 which indicates possible explanations for Khrushchev's actions. Pupils could address these questions in discussion, although a written presentation of their ideas would be a desirable outcome.

Questions 1–3 on page 298 also require similarly high-level thinking. Question 1 addresses the issue of different interpretations of the same event. Clearly provenance is a crucial factor in the difference, as well as the actual tone and content of the sources. Question 2 requires a substantiated opinion, and like questions 1 and 3, could be tackled in a discussion format. Question 3 is particularly suited to discussion. For a little extra support pupils could break the question into stages:

1 Look at Source 28.
   (a) What relevant information does it contain?
   (b) Which points of information can you check as true? How?
   (c) Do these checks make you sure?

2 Look at Source 29.
   (a) What relevant information does it contain?
   (b) Which points of information can you check as true? How?
   (c) Do these checks make you sure?
   (d) Does it help to put the information from Sources 28 and 29 together? Explain.

3 Look at Source 30.
   (a) What relevant information does it contain?
   (b) Which points of information can you check as true? How?
   (c) Do these checks make you sure?
   (d) Does it help to put the information from Sources 28, 29 and 30 together? Explain.

These questions should ensure pupils are well prepared for the Focus Task on page 298. The task requires the synthesis of a range of skills and the application of their knowledge. Worksheet 12.5 sets out a structure for applying those processes. For Part 1, pupils should be directed back to Worksheet 12.2a. Part 2 could be answered in discussion or in writing, although Worksheet 12.5 subsumes the issue into the final written work.

Case-study 3: The Vietnam War

Most pupils will have heard of Vietnam, but probably few will know much about the background to the war. The narrative is purposely detailed, broken up by relatively few sources and maps. The concepts of review and overview arise again in question 1 on page 300. Pupils could benefit from actually drawing up the lists, or applying the ideas of Worksheet 12.5.

The Focus Task on page 300 is aimed at concentrating pupils' minds on the narrative on pages 299–300. It is also a task which involves an analysis of the causal processes. The task is structured to support pupils. As an extension exercise, pupils could draw lines between the events and explain the connections that these lines represent. Part 4 involves pupils undertaking some lateral thinking. It may be most appropriate as a discussion exercise. This could be returned to at the end of the next section, when pupils have looked at the American defeat.

Why did the USA lose the Vietnam War?

This section focuses on the ways in which an apparently small band of impoverished guerrillas was able to defy the might of the USA. The section makes extensive use of sources, but the emphasis is more on extracting relevant information than on assessing reliability. This is best done by cross-referencing the wide range of sources with provenance. Questions 2–4 on page 301 are perhaps best suited to written answers, not least because they raise extremely important issues. However, they could also be used for small-group discussion as preparation for the Focus Task at the top of page 305, dealing with the changing phases of the American involvement in the war.

The Activity on page 304 is a logical extension of this task, essentially an example of applying knowledge in a practical way. Pupils might find the criteria set out in **Worksheet 12.6** helpful. They could even be directed to focus the poster exclusively on the My Lai incident. **Questions 1–3** should prove useful preparation if this option is chosen.

How did the Vietnam War affect the policy of containment?

The chapter is concluded with two **Focus Tasks**. The first addresses the reasons for the US defeat in Vietnam, whereas the second asks pupils to return to the overview.

Worksheet 12.7a and b provide an alternative structure for tackling the first task. Many pupils could move straight from one or other format to a piece of extended writing. However, less confident pupils may find the progression from grid to layout to continuous writing helpful.

The final Focus Task should bring pupils back to **Worksheet 12.2a** and a final overview of the policy of containment. The merits of this policy would be an ideal subject for small-group discussion followed up by a written exercise. An enjoyable exercise is for pupils to work in groups and brainstorm the issue under headings. (Pupils should look beyond the three case-studies.)

- What events were definite successes?
- What were definite failures?
- What seem to fall between?
- List five reasons for successes.
- List five reasons for failures.

These should be written on small pieces of paper and placed in envelopes. Groups should then swap envelopes and try to reconstruct the arrangement using other groups' ideas. Finally, using blackboard, or OHP, teachers could try to pull together a consensus about successes, failures and 'halfway' events. This should form an excellent springboard for an essay. For weaker groups, teachers may wish to prepare cards themselves.

MacArthur is sacked!

12.1

AIM

To describe and explain General MacArthur's actions in Korea

RESOURCES

Read through pages 287–289. In 1951, President Truman removed MacArthur from command of the UN forces. The letter below is MacArthur's chance to explain his actions. Fill in the gaps.

Dear Mr President

I was deeply saddened when I heard that you have removed me from command of forces in Korea. I would like to try to explain my actions.

Firstly I believe in the policy of containment because _____

_____

_____

_____

_____

_____

I also felt that I was fighting for the USA, not the UNO. For example _____

_____

_____

_____

_____

_____

I believed that the aim of the mission was more than to simply rescue South Korea. It was

_____

_____

_____

_____

_____

Invading North Korea was right because

_____

_____

_____

_____

_____

Furthermore, I did not believe the Chinese were such a great threat because

_____

_____

_____

_____

_____

GCSE Modern World History

WORSHEET **12.2a**

Containment in action

Keep this worksheet safe – you will come back to it several times.

AIM

To investigate the policy of containment in the period 1950–1973

RESOURCES

The Korean War

Read over your work on each case-study in this chapter and complete the chart below:

The issue	Methods used by USA	Problems faced	Outcome
Invasion of South Korea			

The Cuban missile crisis

The issue	Methods used by USA	Problems faced	Outcome

The Vietnam War

The issue	Methods used by USA	Problems faced	Outcome

WORSHEET *The Korean War*

12.2b

AIM

To analyse and explain whether the Korean War was a success for containment

RESOURCES

The year is 1952. A new President, Eisenhower, has been elected in the USA. Your task is to write a report for him on what lessons the United States can learn from the war. The key question is: Has the policy of containment been successful in Korea?

1 Look back at Worksheet 12.2a.

2 Your aim is to present a balanced report on the war, divided into the following sections:

- The USA's aims
- How far the aims were achieved
- How the UNO helped
- MacArthur's actions and why he was removed
- The cost of the war.

3 Use the 'pads' below to record your ideas. You should also finish with a conclusion. This should set out

- the ways in which containment succeeded
- how it proved less than successful.

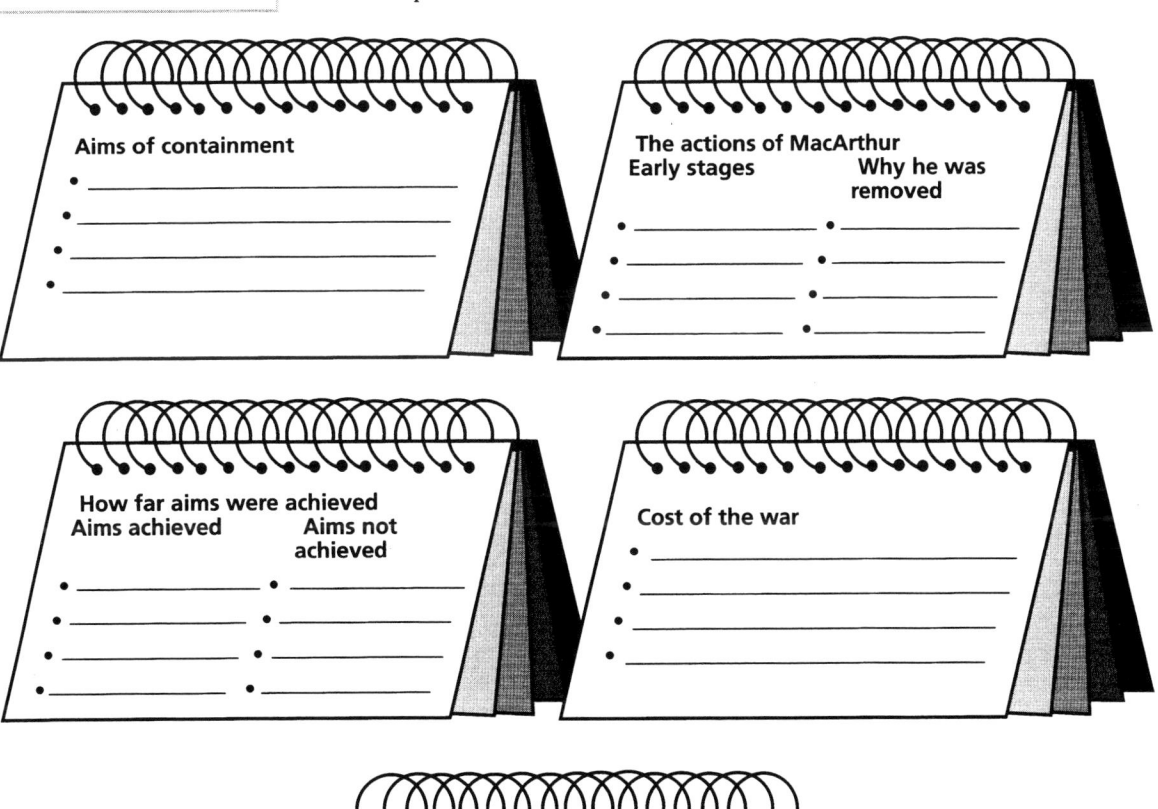

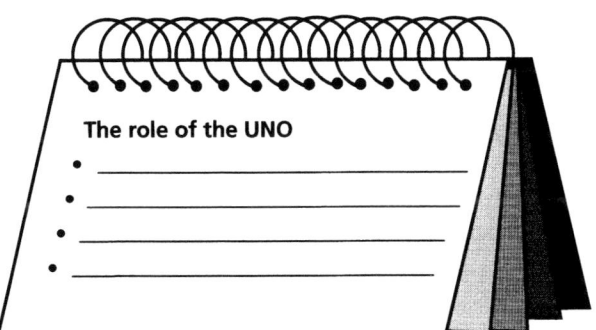

The Cold War in cartoons

AIM

To show an understanding of how historians use political cartoons

RESOURCES

The events of the Cold War offered endless opportunities for cartoonists to try to influence points of view and to make points about each of the sides in the conflict. It can sometimes be difficult to spot all of the points which the cartoonist was trying to make when the cartoon was drawn. Use the following pointers to help you when you look at a cartoon:

Background

- The date it was drawn – what else was going on at the same time?
- The country and the type of publication in which the cartoon was published.

Words

- Look at the caption (if the cartoon has one) – it is usually very blunt.
- Many cartoons use labels on the characters or include objects. Look very carefully for these as they give very strong clues as to what the cartoon is about.

The cartoon itself

- Start by looking at the background if there is one – what sort of impression is it trying to give?
- Look at any figures and think about how the cartoonist has drawn them in terms of size, bulk and their position in relation to each other.
- Facial expressions are usually very important – they tell you whether the cartoonist thinks that a character is brave, cowardly, sincere, treacherous etc.

Your task

1 Choose two cartoons from Chapter 12 which you believe show opposing views in the Cold War. Use the formula above to analyse them, and then write a short commentary on each one.
2 The year is 1949. Work in pairs, one designing a cartoon supporting the West and one supporting the USSR.
   a) Draw your own cartoon supporting your view.
   b) Design a cartoon and write accurate instructions to an artist.

Your cartoon should include:

- a background
- a caption – preferably using sarcasm or humour
- figures who can be clearly recognised
- labels on the cartoon itself to help people understand the point you are trying to make.

Cuba: What should the President do?

AIM

To describe and explain the options available to President Kennedy in 1962

RESOURCES

1 Do nothing?

For: The Americans still had a vastly greater nuclear power than the Soviet Union. The USA could still destroy the Soviet Union, so – the argument went – the USSR would never use these missiles. The biggest danger to world peace would be to overreact to this discovery.

Against: The USSR had lied about Cuban missiles. Kennedy had already issued his solemn warning to the USSR. To do nothing would be another sign of weakness.

2 Surgical air attack?

An immediate selected air attack to destroy the nuclear bases themselves.

For: It would destroy the missiles before they were ready to use.

Against:
1 Destruction of all sites could not be guaranteed. And even one left standing could launch a counter-attack against the USA.
2 The attack would inevitably kill Soviet soldiers. The Soviet Union might retaliate at once.
3 To attack without advance warning was seen as immoral.

5 Blockade?

A ban on the Soviet Union bringing in any further military supplies to Cuba, enforced by the US navy who would stop and search Soviet ships. And a call for the Soviet Union to withdraw what was already there.

For: It would show the USA was serious, but it would not be a direct act of war. It would put the burden on Khrushchev to decide what to do next. The USA had a strong navy and could still take the other options if this one did not work.

Against: It would not solve the main problem – the missiles were already on Cuba. They could be used within one week. The Soviet Union might retaliate by blockading Berlin as they had done in 1948.

3 Diplomatic pressures?

To get the United Nations or other body to intervene and negotiate.

For: It would avoid conflict.

Against: If the USA was forced to back down it would be a sign of weakness.

4 Invasion?

All-out invasion of Cuba by air and sea.

For: An invasion could not only get rid of the missiles but Castro as well. The American forces were already trained and available to do it.

Against: It would almost certainly guarantee an equivalent Soviet response either to protect Cuba or within the Soviet sphere of influence – for example a takeover of Berlin.

Work in small groups. Your task is to look at each of the five options open to the President and advise him about them. You must throw out three options and give him two to choose from.

1 Use the chart below to help you by rating each option in order; 1 means the best option, 5 the worst.

Option	Rating	Explanation for rating
Do nothing		
Surgical air attack		
Diplomatic pressures		
Invasion		
Blockade		

2 Now write a short report for the President, divided into sections:

    1 The two options you believe he should decide between
    2 Why you feel these are the right options
    3 Why you rejected particular options ....

WORSHEET *The Cuban crisis*

12.5

AIM

To investigate the Cuban crisis and explain whether it was a success for containment

RESOURCES

Write an essay, organised in paragraphs, to answer this question:

Was the Cuban missile crisis a success for the USA's policy of containment?

Work through this in stages.

1 Go back to Worksheet 12.2(a), on which you filled out a chart on the Korean War. Now use pages 293–298 to complete the section on the Cuban missile crisis.

2 In small groups, decide on your answers to these questions:

  • In what ways were the two events similar?
  • In what ways were they different?
  • Which of these two events was the greater test for the USA?

  (Give three reasons for your choice)

3 Now plan your essay. The boxes set out the paragraphs which will make up your essay. Look back at your recent work and pages 293–298 and decide which examples and evidence will go into each paragraph. (Remember, you may wish to use the same point twice.)

Paragraph 1:
The Cuban crisis was certainly more of a success for the USA than the Bay of Pigs. (Explain why.)
_____
_____
_____
_____
_____
_____

Paragraph 4:
Kennedy gained a lot from the crisis.
_____
_____
_____
_____
_____
_____
_____

Paragraph 2:
The Cuban missiles posed a serious challenge for the USA because ...
_____
_____
_____
_____
_____
_____

Paragraph 3:
Kennedy had a number of options. These were ...
_____
_____
_____
He chose ... (explain why) _____
_____
_____

Paragraph 5:
Overall, the Cuban missile crisis was not a success for containment because ...
_____
_____
_____
_____
_____
_____
_____

WORSHEET *Vietnam: USA out!*

12.6

AIM

To describe and explain the arguments used by anti-Vietnam protesters in the 1960s

RESOURCES

The year is 1968. You are a student at an American university protesting about US involvement in the Vietnam War. Your task is to create a poster spelling out the reasons why young Americans should not have to fight in Vietnam.

Before you design your poster you will need to do some background research.

In this box, decide what images will be in your poster. Think about:

• background (e.g. destroyed villages)
• the central image (e.g. a picture of a young soldier)
• how you will put across your message (pictures? words? both?).

In this box note down all of the reasons why you feel the war in Vietnam is wrong.

In this box make a note of what you are trying to achieve with this poster (e.g. to convince people to write to their Congressmen to get the troops out).

Try out different slogans.

Why did the USA lose the Vietnam War?

AIM

To evaluate the relative importance of different reasons for the American defeat in Vietnam

RESOURCES

To help you prepare for the Focus Task on page 305 look back at your work on the Vietnam War and pages 299–305 and complete this table.

WHY DID THE USA LOSE THE VIETNAM WAR?

How these factors played a part				
US tactics	Unpopularity of South Vietnamese regime	Quality of Viet Cong and US fighters	Opposition to war in USA	Chinese and Soviet support for Viet Cong
			)	

Why did the USA lose the Vietnam War?

AIM

To evaluate the relative importance of different reasons for the American defeat in Vietnam

RESOURCES

1 Summarise the importance of each factor in the boxes below.

2 Give each factor a mark out of ten for its importance.

3 To show related causes, either
   a) draw lines to show links
   b) colour/shade them.

4 Explain the grouping or links you have made.

US tactics	Mark /10

Opposition to war in USA	Mark /10

Chinese and Soviet support for Viet Cong	Mark /10

WHY DID THE USA LOSE THE VIETNAM WAR?

Unpopularity of South Vietnamese regime	Mark /10

Quality of Viet Cong and US fighters	Mark /10

The Red Empire in eastern Europe 1948–1989

13

Key features of the chapter

	Issue(s) covered	Assessment elements	Format(s) for pupil work
Focus Task (p.308): 1953	Stalin's impact on eastern Europe	Selecting and deploying information	Obituary for Stalin
Activity (p.310): Hungary 1956	Reasons for uprising	Use of sources, selecting and deploying information	Letter from Imre Nagy to Eisenhower
Focus Task (p.311): Suppression of the uprising	How strong was Soviet control?	Analysing events	Comparison of different views
Focus Task (p.314): Rebellions	Comparison of Hungary 1956 and Czechoslovakia 1968	Analyse and explain events	Written report
Focus Task (p.317): Berlin Wall	Why did the Communists build the Berlin Wall?	Analyse and explain events, use of sources	Report
Focus Task (p.321): Solidarity	Impact of Solidarity	Selecting and deploying knowledge	Substantiated writing
Activity (p.322): How did Gorbachev change eastern Europe?	Role of Gorbachev	Use of sources	Extended profile of Gorbachev
Focus Task (p.324): Gorbachev's reforms	Why were reforms needed?	The key features of an historical situation	A poster
Focus Task (p.327): Gorbachev	Gorbachev and eastern Europe	Use of sources, selecting and deploying knowledge	Letter and report

The Issue Starter

With these questions in mind, pupils should be able to read through the chapter with a purpose. To get to the heart of the matter, they could be encouraged to look at **Source 2**, which establishes the all-important geography of eastern Europe. Pupils will find the complex goings on in eastern Europe far easier to understand if they have a grasp of the geography of the area. This might even be the basis of a learn and test exercise, extended with some reference work. **Worksheet 13.1** provides a template for this overview exercise, which could be regarded as valuable 'investment time'.

How secure was Stalin's control of eastern Europe?

This section aims to introduce the notion of a Soviet monolith, while at the same time pointing out to pupils the inherent weaknesses in the system. Pupils might find it helpful to look at **Source 1** and carry out an analysis of it. Following that, they should read the accompanying text. It is a good example of how the context of a primary source can help in clarifying its meaning.

Question 1 on page 307 asks pupils to show their grasp of Stalin's carrot and stick approach by extracting relevant examples from the Factfiles and text. They might find it helpful to use a simple table such as this:

Date	Examples of carrots	Examples of sticks

As soon as the notion of the monolith is set up, it is important that pupils begin to question it. An ideal way to raise this doubt is through a discussion of **questions 1–3** on **page 308** on the case of Tito in Yugoslavia. **Source 4** is deliberately provided with an extensive provenance but the questions are mainly to encourage critical thinking. Pupils need to apply their knowledge and find reasons to substantiate any judgements they make.

Once these are completed, they should be ready to tackle the **Focus Task** on **page 308**. This is actually a challenging task, requiring some deep thinking and some rigorous organisation of material. For pupils needing help, **Worksheet 13.2** provides a frame for the obituary.

How was Khrushchev different from Stalin?

This section is short but highly significant. Pupils must gain an understanding of people's perceptions of Khrushchev in eastern Europe, in order to understand perceptions from 1956 onwards. As a review activity, they could draw up a table to help them organise their thoughts:

Area	Khrushchev	Stalin
Background and upbringing (Profiles, pages 99 and 309)		
Party career (Profiles, pages 99 and 309)		
Views on Communism and eastern Europe (pages 98–108 and 306–311)		

How did the Soviet Union deal with opposition in eastern Europe?

Pupils will recognise the relevance of the previous section as they look at the early rumblings in East Germany and Poland. The issue of opposition in eastern Europe is dealt with through two key case-studies – Hungary in 1956 and Czechoslovakia in 1968.

Case-study 1: Hungary, 1956

Questions 1 and 2 on page 310 might be best addressed in a written form, although they might also be used as discussion questions in preparation for the **Activity** which follows.
Sources 8–10 carry an enormous amount of information and detail – question 1 certainly merits feedback on a whole-class basis so that such detail is not missed. Question 2 requires pupils to think back to the **Focus Task** on **page 308**, the obituary of Stalin. By reviewing the mechanics of Stalin's

control of eastern Europe, they should be able to recognise the worries caused by Hungarian demands. Above all, of course, they must stress the question of the Warsaw Pact and how it would threaten Soviet security.

The **Activity** is an application of this information and knowledge – pupils should process information rather than simply moving it from the textbook to their files or exercise books. They need to organise their findings from the previous two questions under the headings provided in the Activity.

Questions 3–6 on page 311 require a detailed study of the events of the uprising. It would be best if pupils collaborated on them, and were then supported by teacher feedback. The cross-referencing of **Sources 11–14** is a vitally important skill. Some pupils might find an alternative line of enquiry profitable:

1 What two main points arise in Source 11?
2 What new information does Source 12 give you?
3 Has your view of the situation changed after using two sources?
4 What new information does Source 13 give you?
5 Which points above does Source 14 support?
6 'Four sources provide a better picture of events than just one.' Explain why this is true.

Questions 7 and 8 are more reflective and discursive. Their aim is to lay the ground for the demanding **Focus Task** at the end of this sub-section. **Worksheet 13.3** provides a visual structure to help pupils produce a balanced response. They need to look at a number of broad areas:

• The underlying reasons for discontent
• The demands of the rebels
• The fierceness of the fighting
• The attitude of the West.

Once they have grasped these areas, pupils must then decide how the evidence can support one or both statements. The task is well suited to a group-work approach followed up by individual written work.

Case-study 2: Czechoslovakia and the Prague Spring, 1968

This section deals with the Prague Spring, but it is also a vehicle for the comparative study in the **Focus Task** on **page 314**. This is foreshadowed in the questions on **page 312**. In **question 1**, pupils are asked to extract relevant information from written sources, whereas **question 2** asks them to recall their work on Hungary. Some pupils may find this difficult, so it may be helpful to introduce them to the Focus Task as soon as they start the section and use **Worksheet 13.4** to help them keep abreast of events.

The table format offers the extra opportunity to turn this visual overview into extended writing, or a class discussion. The Focus Task suggests a slightly more personalised approach to a follow-up task, but the rigour remains. Pupils must still isolate key areas and substantiate any views expressed with examples.

Why was the Berlin Wall built?

As in the previous section, pupils will find it helpful if the Focus Task is 'flagged up' in advance of them working through the section. The section opens with a Communist cartoon, and **questions 1 and 2** on **page 314** are discussion questions aimed at bringing pupils to the heart of the issue. Looking across the pages, there is an obvious discrepancy between the messages of **Sources 24 and 27**.

Question 3 on page 315 is a discussion question, although it may be valuable for pupils to write up their views on the two photographs once they have discussed them. With the Focus Task in mind, the remainder of the section relies heavily on a series of visual images. This should help pupils to plan and carry out the Focus Task on page 317. The poster form of presentation is used because posters were one of the most prominent forms of protest used at the time. It is important that pupils plan and produce the poster carefully. Some may prefer to write a briefing for an artist. A useful extension exercise is for pupils to write a short commentary on their poster. Alternatively they might explain what questions they would set on it, if their poster appeared in a textbook. Worksheet 13.5 provides support for the task.

Why did the Cold War thaw in the 1970s?

This issue is dealt with in brief through the seminal Source 33. Although not a central issue, the question of detente forms an important background to the chapter. The aim of Source 33 is to try to summarise the 'ingredients' of detente and the ways in which it affected the USSR. In turn, anything affecting the USSR inevitably affected eastern Europe.

Why was Solidarity a threat to Soviet control?

The history of Solidarity is used as a case-study to chart the rise of opposition to Communism in Poland. From this, pupils should be able to draw out the logical implications of events in Poland for Soviet control of the rest of eastern Europe.

Question 1 on page 319 is a straightforward comprehension exercise, but it does ask pupils to focus on how style and tone convey as important a message as actual words. Question 1 on page 320 similarly looks at use of language. Together, the two questions should establish in pupils' minds the nature of the Polish government in the early 1980s.

Worksheet 13.6 is designed to help pupils tackle the Focus Task on page 321. Although the task is based around the timeline on page 319, pupils must read the accompanying text and sources on pages 319–321 if they are to complete it effectively.

How did Gorbachev change eastern Europe?

Mikhail Gorbachev is a remarkable example of how a politician can undergo a meteoric rise on the world stage and fall into decline almost as quickly. The opening source-based activity aims to help pupils grasp the immense impact of Gorbachev's new attitude to the USSR's government, as well as its relations with the USA. There is a good deal of information in Sources 37–45 and pupils may well wish to work in groups and divide the workload. They may find the recording template on Worksheet 13.7 useful.

Why did Soviet control of eastern Europe collapse?

Like Source 33 on detente, this section contains essential background information. Without a grasp of events in the USSR, pupils will struggle to follow the collapse of Soviet control in eastern Europe.

Source 49 is the seminal source of the section and the **Activity** aims to make sure that pupils understand the sequence of events. In order to avoid copying, pupils must go through a process of identifying key events and summarising them. **Worksheet 13.8** provides an outline for the timeline, although pupils may well come up with their own ideas for a format.

Worksheet 13.8 also links closely to the **Focus Task** at the end of the chapter. As always, the Focus Task requires an application of knowledge gained and some lateral thinking about the sources and information pupils have read. **Worksheet 13.9** provides some guidance.

Eastern Europe – an overview

AIM

To become familiar with the countries of eastern Europe

RESOURCES

It is easy to become confused between all the different countries and cities in eastern Europe. Use the map below to gain a familiarity with them.

1 Skim read through the chapter (you may wish to use the index at the back of the book) and find out where each state is.
2 In each box, note down three important events concerning that state.
3 Also in the box, note down on which pages the country is mentioned.

Key

▨ Territory taken over by USSR at end of Second World War

▥ Soviet-dominated Communist governments

▤ Other Communist governments

EAST GERMANY	POLAND	CZECHOSLOVAKIA	HUNGARY
Key events	**Key events**	**Key events**	**Key events**
•	•	•	•
•	•	•	•
•	•	•	•
Mentioned on pages	**Mentioned on pages**	**Mentioned on pages**	**Mentioned on pages**

WORKSHEET

13.2

Stalin and eastern Europe

AIM

To describe and explain how Stalin controlled eastern Europe

RESOURCES

It is 1953. Stalin has died and your task is to write part of a detailed obituary for him. The job given to you is to explain his control over eastern Europe.

Use the writing frame below to help you.

1 Stalin controlled eastern Europe with an iron grip. At the end of the war, several factors helped him to put Communists into power :

_____

_____

_____

_____

_____

2 Once Communists were in power, Stalin kept close control of them.
Through Comecon he :

_____

_____

Through Cominform he _____

_____

_____

_____

3 There were challenges to Stalin, and not all of eastern Europe submitted to him. For example . . .

_____

_____

_____

_____

_____

_____

_____

_____

The Hungarian uprising

AIM

To analyse and explain the strength of Soviet control of Hungary in 1956

RESOURCES

Focus question

Do the events of 1956 in Hungary show the strength or the weakness of Soviet control over Hungary?

1 Opposition to Rakosi → 2 Rakosi not supported by Moscow → 3 Rakosi removed

6 Imre Nagy forms new government ← 5 Soviet tanks move in and then withdraw ← 4 Rebellion

7 Nagy's plans → 8 Khrushchev sends in troops → 9 Two weeks of fierce street fighting → 10 Nagy imprisoned and executed

1 Look carefully at the flow chart above and read pages 310–311.

2 Now complete the table below. For each event, decide whether it supports the view that Soviet control was weak or strong. There may be some events which could be used to support either view. You may also wish to add extra events.

Events which suggest strong Soviet control (explain)	Events which suggest weak Soviet control (explain)	Events which fall in between (explain)

3 Use your table to put together some paragraphs with the title 'The evidence presents a contrasting picture about the events in Hungary in 1956'.

Paragraph 1: When we look at the events in Hungary in 1956 it seems sensible to think that the USSR was in complete control. This is because _____

_____

_____

Paragraph 2: However, when we look at events from a different viewpoint the picture is not so clear. If Soviet control was so strong, surely these events would have been impossible. For example:

_____

_____

WORKSHEET

13.4

The challenge to Communist rule – 1

GCSE Modern World History

AIM

To identify and describe the similarities and differences between the Hungarian and Czech uprisings

RESOURCES

Read through pages 310–313 and think about the ways in which the rebellions were similar and the ways in which they were different. Use the table below to record what you find out.

Issues	Hungary	Czechoslovakia	Conclusion – similar or different (give reasons)?
The aims of the rebels			
Attitude towards Communism			
Attitude towards democracy			
Attitude to the USSR			
Attitude to the West			
Why the Soviet Union intervened			
How each state responded to Soviet intervention			
Eventual outcome			

EXTENSION WORK

It is 1968. You are a Hungarian opponent of the Communists. You were thrown out in 1956 and since then you have been illegally broadcasting uncensored news to eastern European countries from West Germany. You have now sneaked into Czechoslovakia to find out about events first-hand.

Write a report, of about 200 words, explaining how events in Czechoslovakia compare with your own experiences in 1956 in Hungary.

You will find the table above gives you a structure for your report.

Why was the Berlin Wall built?

13.5

AIM

To show an understanding of reactions to the building of the Wall, and why people believed it was built

RESOURCES

Work in pairs. Make a poster or notice to be stuck on the Berlin Wall explaining the purpose of the Wall and what the results of the wall will be. One of you should make a poster to show the official East German view and the other to show the view of the West.

Each poster must be carefully planned, and you need to search through pages 314–317 for pictures and quotations.

Before you design your poster you will need to do some background research.

In this box, decide what images will be in your poster. Think about:
- background (e.g. separated families; people killed trying to cross the Wall)
- the central image (e.g. a picture of a checkpoint)
- how you will put across your message (pictures? words? both?).

In this box note down all of the reasons why you feel the Wall was built.

In this box make a note of what you are trying to achieve with this poster.

Try out different slogans.

WORSHEET *Solidarity*

WORKSHEET

13.6

Between August 1980 and December 1981 Solidarity went through some rapid changes. Some were particularly important in the rise and fall of Solidarity.

1 On the graph below, decide where each event belongs on the importance scale.

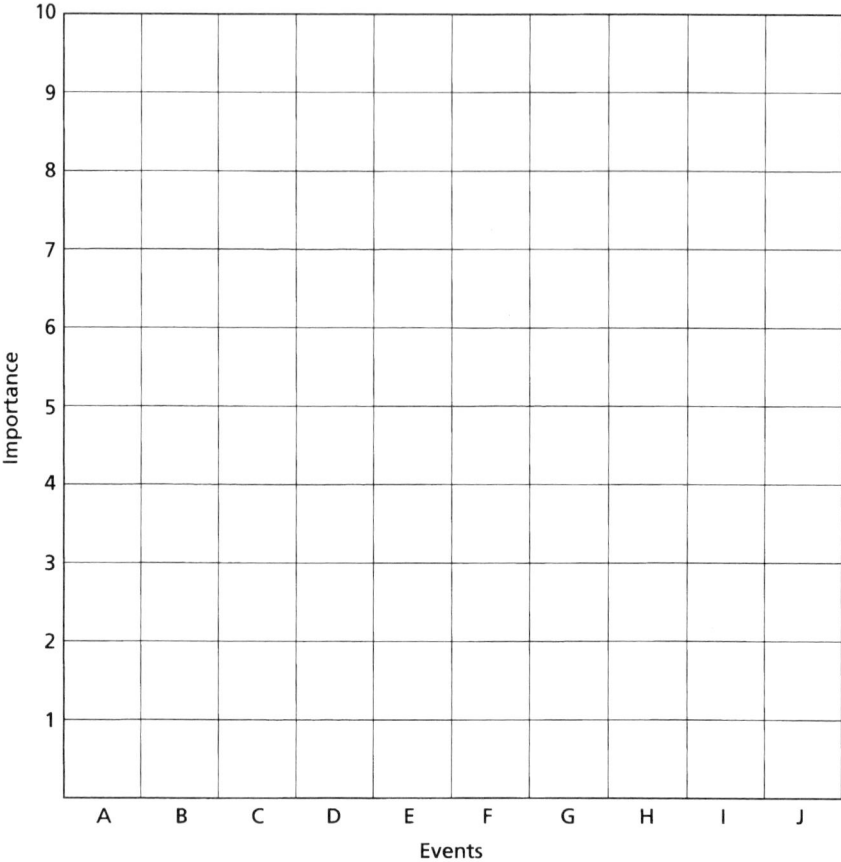

A August 1980 Solidarity is founded
B 30 August Government agrees to Solidarity demands
C October 1980 Solidarity recognised by government
D January 1981 Solidarity membership reaches peak of 9.4 million
E February 1981 Jaruzelski becomes Polish leader
F March 1981 Bydgoszcz strike called off
G May 1981 Rural Solidarity set up
H September 1981 Open letter to workers of eastern Europe
I November 1981 Negotiations between Jaruzelski and Walesa break down
J December 1981 Martial law in Poland

2 Choose the two events with the highest rating on your graph and explain why you have put them there.

AIM

To describe and explain the changing position of Solidarity in 1980–1981

RESOURCES

EXTENSION WORK

Write an answer, organised in paragraphs, to the following question:
'Solidarity was important, but only in Poland.' How far do you agree with this statement?

Paragraph 1: Your overall view
Paragraph 2: Why Solidarity was so successful
Paragraph 3: How Solidarity was important in Poland (use examples, such as negotiating with the government)
Paragraph 4: Why the USSR was concerned about Solidarity
Paragraph 5: Your conclusion.

What was Gorbachev like?

Sources 37–45 on pages 322–323 are all extracts from letters sent to Mikhail Gorbachev in the late 1980s. From these letters, work out as much as you can about Gorbachev. You could work in groups and split the work up among pairs. When you have finished, report back. As a group complete the table.

<table>
<thead>
<tr><th>Source</th><th>What kind of person was Gorbachev?</th><th>What changes did he introduce to the USSR? disarmament?</th><th>What was his policy on eastern Europe?</th><th>What was his attitude to nuclear issues?</th><th>What did he think about environmental</th><th>What did he think about human rights?</th></tr>
</thead>
<tbody>
<tr><td>Source 37</td><td></td><td></td><td></td><td></td><td></td><td></td></tr>
<tr><td>Source 38</td><td></td><td></td><td></td><td></td><td></td><td></td></tr>
<tr><td>Source 39</td><td></td><td></td><td></td><td></td><td></td><td></td></tr>
<tr><td>Source 40</td><td></td><td></td><td></td><td></td><td></td><td></td></tr>
<tr><td>Source 41</td><td></td><td></td><td></td><td></td><td></td><td></td></tr>
<tr><td>Source 42</td><td></td><td></td><td></td><td></td><td></td><td></td></tr>
<tr><td>Source 43</td><td></td><td></td><td></td><td></td><td></td><td></td></tr>
<tr><td>Source 44</td><td></td><td></td><td></td><td></td><td></td><td></td></tr>
<tr><td>Source 45</td><td></td><td></td><td></td><td></td><td></td><td></td></tr>
</tbody>
</table>

AIM

To use a range of written sources to assess the character and impact of Mikhail Gorbachev

RESOURCES

THE RED EMPIRE IN EASTERN EUROPE 1948–1989

WORKSHEET

13.8

The collapse of Communism

GCSE Modern World History

AIM

To identify the main events of 1989 in eastern Europe

RESOURCES

Look at Source 49 and read through pages 325–327 carefully. In pairs, decide which ten events or points you will put on the timeline below. Remember, your aim is to identify the sequence of events in 1989.

WORSHEET

13.9

The challenge to Communist rule – 2

AIM

To describe and explain why Communism collapsed in 1989 and the importance of Gorbachev in that process

RESOURCES

Focus question

As you work through the activities below, keep thinking about this question:

How far was Gorbachev responsible for the collapse of Soviet control in eastern Europe?

1 Read Source 46 on page 324 carefully.
a) You have to explain Source 46 to someone who has not seen it. Summarise what Gorbachev says in three simple points.
b) Explain how this attitude would have been seen by Stalin, Khrushchev and Brezhnev, if they had been around to see it.

2 Write a 'Dear Mr Gorbachev' letter responding to Source 46 from either:
a) a member of Solidarity in Poland
b) a supporter of Dubček's reforms in Czechoslovakia in 1968
c) a student who took part in the Hungarian uprising.

3 Either:
a) Write your own 'Dear Mr Gorbachev' letter explaining how far you feel Gorbachev was responsible for the collapse of Soviet control in eastern Europe
or
b) Write an essay of about 250–300 words answering the focus question at the top of the page.

For either option, you need to think carefully about the following questions:

• Did Gorbachev simply 'remove the prop' which set off the collapse of Communism?
• Did Gorbachev not care about eastern Europe, because he was too concerned with the USSR?
• Would the eastern European regimes have collapsed if it had not been for Gorbachev?

Use the notepads below to note down the points you will make.

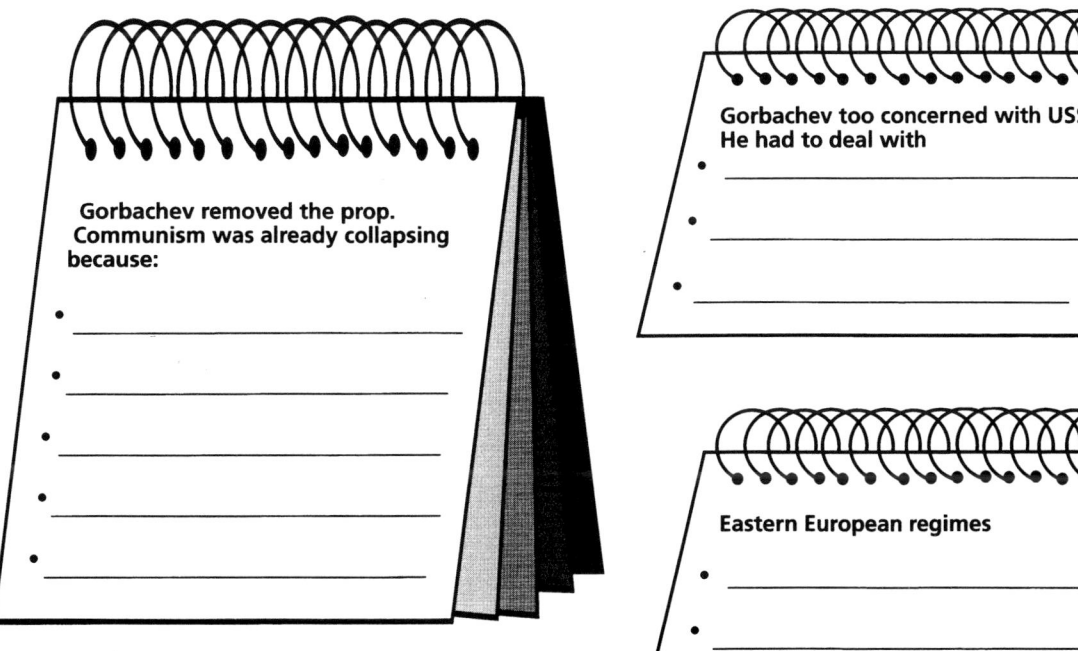

Gorbachev removed the prop. Communism was already collapsing because:

• _____
• _____
• _____
• _____
• _____

Gorbachev too concerned with USSR. He had to deal with

• _____
• _____
• _____

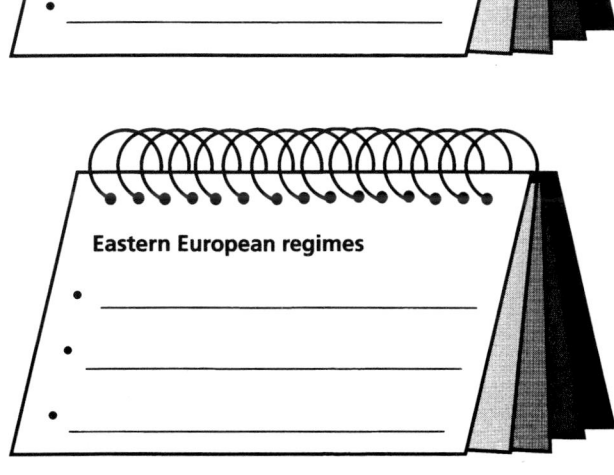

Eastern European regimes

• _____
• _____
• _____